# DESIGN THINKING
## UNDERSTANDING HOW DESIGNERS THINK AND WORK

Nigel Cross

B L O O M S B U R Y

LONDON • NEW DELHI • NEW YORK • SYDNEY

**Bloomsbury Academic**
An imprint of Bloomsbury Publishing Plc

50 Bedford Square      1385 Broadway
London      New York
WC1B 3DP      NY 10018
UK      USA

**www.bloomsbury.com**

**Bloomsbury is a registered trade mark of Bloomsbury Publishing Plc**

English edition first published in 2011 by Berg
Reprinted by Bloomsbury Academic 2013

**British Library Cataloguing-in-Publication Data**
A catalogue record for this book is available from the British Library.

ISBN: HB: 978-1-8478-8637-8
PB: 978-1-8478-8636-1

**Library of Congress Cataloging-in-Publication Data**
A catalog record for this book is available from the Library of Congress.

Typeset by JS Typesetting Ltd, Porthcawl, Mid Glamorgan
Printed and bound in Great Britain

# CONTENTS

# Acknowledgements

My friends Gordon Murray and Kenneth Grange freely and readily gave the time and patience to discuss their work with me, reported in Chapters 2 and 3. Victor Scheinman generously volunteered to participate in the experiment reported in Chapter 5, as did the anonymous designers Ivan, John and Kerry, reported in Chapter 6, all providing their time and talent free of charge, and allowing their design activity to be observed, recorded and analysed. My colleagues at the Delft University of Technology, Kees Dorst and Henri Christiaans, provided the initiative and the hard work in the design and conduct of the experiments. The facilities for the experiments were provided by the Xerox Palo Alto Research Center, with the help of Steve Harrison and Scott Minneman. My wife Anita also contributed to analysing the experiments, to discussions with Gordon and Kenneth, and to my general well-being.

# Introduction

In writing this book, my goal has been to help anyone interested in design to develop their understanding of how designers think and work. Anyone so interested might be a design student, a design researcher or teacher, a manager in a design-oriented company, or even a designer who still finds their own processes mysterious or difficult. The focus of the book is on revealing what designers do during the activity of designing, and on building an understanding of the nature of design ability. Readers should gain from the book some insight into what it means to be a designer, how designers employ creative thinking skills, and what is known about different aspects of design ability and its development from novice student to expert professional.

My own background includes architecture and industrial design, but primarily I am a design researcher with an interest in the common aspects of designing that recur across different professional domains of practice. My approach to trying to understand how designers think and work is research-based: I look for and report evidence that comes from observation, experiment, analysis and reflection. My aim is to reveal and articulate the apparently mysterious (and sometimes deliberately mystified) cognitive and creative abilities of designers, that are common across many design domains.

At the core of the book is a number of case studies, each treated in depth as a complete chapter. These are interlaced with chapters that summarise and discuss what can be learned from the case studies in more general terms, and from the research literature of studies of design cognition. The case studies provide a focused resource for the study of high-quality design thinking. The summary and overview chapters provide discussion and reflection that I hope lead the reader into a deeper understanding of the nature of design thinking. This not a 'methods' or 'how-to' book, but a book that reveals what has been learned from research into many different aspects of design thinking. It is a book that provides commentary and advice, rather than instruction.

The first two case studies (Chapters 2 and 3) are interview-based, and draw upon the work of famous, contemporary, outstanding designers: one an automotive designer, and the other a product designer. Another two case studies (Chapters 5 and 6) are experiment-based research studies, using an expert engineering designer and a small, high-quality product design team each tackling the same project in a recorded, laboratory situation. In addition to the observations to be made, and lessons to be drawn from these particular case studies, I draw upon the research literature in order to amplify and extend from the particular to the general.

I take an interdisciplinary approach to design, so throughout the book observations are made, and comparisons are drawn, across various professional fields such as architecture, product, engineering and automotive design. Other professional design domains, such as computer software and interaction design, furniture, textiles and graphic design are also mentioned. But because I take a research-based approach to understanding design thinking, some domains get less coverage in the book simply because less research has been conducted in them. Nevertheless, I believe that many aspects of design thinking are common across the different domains, and so I trust that my observations and comments will be valid across them all.

# 1

# Design Ability

Our job is to give the client, on time and on cost, not what he wants, but what he never dreamed he wanted; and when he gets it, he recognises it as something he wanted all the time.

Denys Lasdun, architect.

Everyone can – and does – design. We all design when we plan for something new to happen, whether that might be a new version of a recipe, a new arrangement of the living room furniture, or a new layout of a personal web page. The evidence from different cultures around the world, and from designs created by children as well as by adults, suggests that everyone is capable of designing. So design thinking is something inherent within human cognition; it is a key part of what makes us human.

We human beings have a long history of design thinking, as evidenced in the artefacts of previous civilisations and in the continuing traditions of vernacular design and traditional craftwork. Everything that we have around us has been designed. Anything that isn't a simple, untouched piece of nature has been designed by someone. The quality of that design effort therefore profoundly affects our quality of life. The ability of designers to produce effective, efficient, imaginative and stimulating designs is therefore important to all of us.

To design things is normal for human beings, and 'design' has not always been regarded as something needing special abilities. Design ability used to be somehow a collective or shared ability, and it is only in fairly recent times that the ability to design has become regarded as a kind of exceptional talent. In traditional, craft-based societies the conception, or 'designing', of artefacts is not really separate from making them; that is to say, there is usually no prior activity of drawing or modelling before the activity of making the artefact. For example, a potter will make a pot by working directly with the clay, and without first making any sketches or drawings of the pot. In modern, industrial societies, however, the activities of designing and of making artefacts are usually quite separate. The process of making something does not normally start before the process of designing it is complete.

Although there is so much design activity going on in the world, the ways in which people design were rather poorly understood for rather a long time. Design ability has been regarded as something that perhaps many people possess to some degree, but only a few people have a particularly strong design 'gift'. Of course, we know that some people are better designers than others. Ever since the emergence of designers as professionals, it has appeared that some people have a design ability that is more highly developed than other people – either through some genetic endowment or through social and educational development. In fact, some people are very good at designing. However, there are now growing bodies of knowledge about the nature of designing, and about the core features or aspects of design ability.

Through research and study there has been a slow but nonetheless steady growth in our understanding of design ability. The kinds of methods for researching the nature of design ability that have been used have included:

■ *Interviews with designers*
These have usually been with designers who are acknowledged as having well-developed design ability, and the methods have usually been conversations or interviews that sought to obtain these designers' reflections on the processes and procedures they use – either in general, or with reference to particular works of design.

■ *Observations and case studies*
These have usually been focused on one particular design project at a time, with observers recording the progress and development of the project either contemporaneously or post hoc. Both participant and non-participant observation methods have been included, and varieties of real, artificially constructed and even re-constructed design projects have been studied.

■ *Experimental studies*
More formal experimental methods have usually been applied to artificial projects, because of the stringent requirements of recording the data. They include asking the experiment participants to 'think aloud' as they respond to a given design task. These statements and the associated actions of the participants are sub-divided into short 'protocols' for analysis. Both experienced designers and inexperienced (often student) designers have been studied in this way.

■ *Simulation*
A relatively new development in research methodology has been the attempt of artificial intelligence (AI) researchers to simulate human thinking through artificial intelligence techniques. Although AI techniques may be meant to supplant human thinking, research in AI can also be a means of trying to understand human thinking.

■ *Reflection and theorising*
As well as the empirical research methods listed above, there has been a significant history in design research of theoretical analysis and reflection upon the nature of design ability.

We therefore have a varied set of methods that have been used for research into design ability. The set ranges from the more concrete to the more abstract types of investigation, and from the more close to the more distant study of actual design practice. The studies have ranged through inexperienced or student designers, to experienced and expert designers, and even to forms of non-human, artificial intelligence. All of these methods have helped researchers to develop insights into what has been referred to as 'designerly' ways of thinking.

The use of a variety of research methods has been required because to understand design ability it is necessary to approach it slightly obliquely. Like all kinds of sophisticated cognitive abilities, it is impossible to approach it directly, or bluntly. For example, designers themselves are often not very good at explaining how they design. When designers – especially skilled, successful designers – talk spontaneously about what they do, they talk almost exclusively about the outcomes, not the activities. They talk about the products of their designing, rather than the process. This is a common feature of experts in any field. Their enthusiasm lies in evaluating what they produce, and not in analysing how they produce it.

Sometimes, some designers can even seem to be wilfully obscure about how they work, and where their ideas come from. The renowned (perhaps even notorious) French designer Philippe Starck is known to suggest that design ideas seem to come to him quite magically, as if from nowhere. He has said that he has designed a chair while sitting in an aircraft during take-off, in the few minutes while the 'fasten seat belts' sign was still on. Perhaps the instruction to 'fasten seat belts' was an inspirational challenge to his designing. Of the design process of his iconic lemon squeezer for the Italian kitchenware manufacturer Alessi, he has said that, in a restaurant, 'this vision of a squid-like lemon squeezer came upon me ...' And so, *Juicy Salif*, the lemon squeezer (Figure 1.1), was conceived, went into production and on to become a phenomenally successful product in terms of sales (if not necessarily in terms of its apparent function).

Designers can also seem to be quite arrogant in the claims that they make. Perhaps it seems arrogant for the architect Denys Lasdun to have claimed

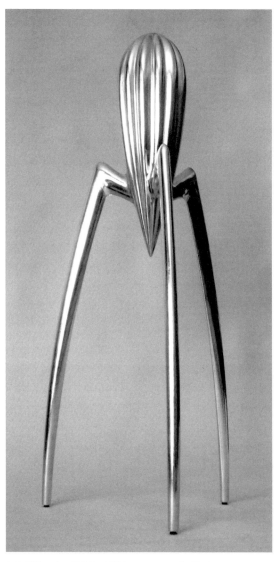

**1.1** Philippe Starck's 'Juicy Salif' lemon squeezer for Alessi.

that 'Our job is to give the client ... *not* what he wants, but what he never dreamed he wanted ...' But I think that we should try to see through the apparent arrogance in this statement, to the underlying truth that clients do want designers to transcend the obvious and the mundane, and to produce proposals which are exciting and stimulating as well as merely practical. What this means is that designing is not a search for the optimum solution to the given problem, but that it is an exploratory process. The creative designer interprets the design brief not as a specification for a solution, but as a starting point for a journey of exploration; the designer sets off to explore, to discover something new, rather than to reach somewhere already known, or to return with yet another example of the already familiar.

I do not want to imply here that designing is indeed a mysterious process, but I do want to suggest that it is complex. Although everyone can design, designing is one of the highest forms of human intelligence. Expert designers exercise very developed forms of certain tacit, deep-seated cognitive skills. But, as we shall see later, it is possible to unravel even Philippe Starck's visionary *Juicy Salif* moment into a much less mysterious explanation in terms of the context of the task he was undertaking, and of the iconography upon which Starck drew for inspiration.

## Asking Designers about what they Do

The spontaneous comments of designers themselves about designing can seem obscure, but it is possible to gain some insights by interviewing them more carefully, and interpreting the implications of their responses. Asking designers about what they do is perhaps the simplest and most direct form of inquiry into design ability, although this technique has not in fact been practised extensively.

Robert Davies interviewed members of the UK-based 'Faculty of Royal Designers for Industry'. This is an élite body of designers, affiliated to The Royal Society for the Encouragement of Arts, Manufactures and Commerce, or the Royal Society of Arts (RSA) as it is more conveniently known. The number of Royal Designers for Industry (RDIs) is limited to a maximum of 100 at any given time, and they are selected for the honour of appointment to the Faculty on the basis of their outstanding achievements in design. So choosing RDIs for interview is one way of ensuring that you are interviewing eminent designers with a record of achievement and accomplishment; that they do indeed possess and use a high level of design ability. At the time Davies conducted his interviews there were sixty-eight RDIs, ranging over professions such as graphic design, product design, furniture design, textile design, fashion design, engineering design, automotive design and interior design. He interviewed thirty-five of these, conducting the interviews informally at their own homes or places of work, but video-recording the discussions.

Davies was especially interested in the creative aspects of design ability, focusing on asking the designers how they thought that they came up with creative insights or concepts. But his informal interviews tended to range widely over many aspects of the design process, and on what seems to make some people 'creative'. One theme that recurred in their responses was the designers' reliance on what they regarded as 'intuition', and on the importance of an 'intuitive' approach. For example, the architect and industrial designer Jack Howe said, 'I believe in intuition. I think that's the difference between a designer and an engineer ... I make a distinction between engineers and engineering designers ... An engineering designer is just as creative as any other sort of designer.' This belief in 'intuition' seems surprising in someone like Jack Howe, whose design work consistently looked rather austere and apparently very rational. The product designer Richard Stevens made a rather similar comment about the difference between engineering and designing: 'A lot of engineering design is intuitive, based on subjective thinking. But an engineer is unhappy doing this. An engineer wants to test; test and measure. He's been brought up this way and he's unhappy if he can't prove something. Whereas an industrial designer, with an Art School training, is entirely happy making judgements which are intuitive.'

What these designers are saying is that they find some aspects of their work appear to them to be natural, perhaps almost unconscious, ways of thinking, and they find that some other types of people (notably, the engineers with whom they come into contact in the course of their work) are uncomfortable with this way of thinking. They believe that this 'intuitive' way of thinking may be something that they inherently possess, or it may be something that they developed through their education. Making decisions, or generating proposals, in the design process is something that they feel relaxed about, and for which they feel no need to seek rational explanations or justifications. But it may be that they are overlooking the experience that they have gathered, and in fact their 'intuitive' responses may be derived from these large pools of experience, and from prior learning gained from making appropriate, and inappropriate, responses in certain situations. We all behave intuitively at times, when we respond in situations that are familiar.

However, designers are perhaps right to call their thinking 'intuitive' in a more profound sense, meaning that it is not based upon conventional forms of logical inferences. The concept of 'intuition' is a convenient, shorthand word for what really happens in design thinking. The more useful concept that has been used by design researchers in explaining the reasoning processes of designers is that design thinking is abductive: a type of reasoning different from the more familiar concepts of inductive and deductive reasoning, but which is the necessary logic of design. It is this particular logic of design that provides the means to shift and transfer thought between the required purpose or function of some activity and appropriate forms for an object to satisfy that purpose. We will explore this logic of design later.

Another theme that emerged from Davies's interviews with these leading designers is related to this tricky relationship between the 'problem' (what is required) and its 'solution' (how to satisfy that). Designers recognise that problems and solutions in design are closely interwoven, that 'the solution' is not always a straightforward answer to 'the problem'. A solution may be something that not only the client, but also the designer 'never dreamed he wanted'. For example, commenting on one of his more creative designs, the furniture designer Geoffrey Harcourt said, 'As a matter of fact, the solution that I came up with wasn't a solution to the problem at all. I never saw it as that ... But when the chair was actually put together, in a way it quite well solved the problem, but from a completely different angle, a completely different point of view.' This comment suggests something of the perceptual aspect of design thinking – like seeing the vase rather than the faces, in the well-known ambiguous figure (Figure 1.2a). It implies that designing utilises aspects of emergence; relevant features emerge in tentative solution concepts, and can be recognised as having properties that suggest how the developing solution-concept might be matched to the also developing problem-concept. Emergent properties are those that are perceived, or recognised, in a partial solution, or a prior solution, that were not consciously included or intended. In a sketch, for example, an emergent aspect is something that was not drawn as itself, but which can be seen in the overlaps or relationships between the drawn components (Figure 1.2b). In the process of designing, the problem and the solution develop together.

Given the complex nature of design activity, therefore, it hardly seems surprising that the structural engineering designer Ted Happold suggested to Davies that, 'I really have, perhaps, one real talent, which is that I don't mind at all living in the area of total uncertainty.' Happold certainly needed this

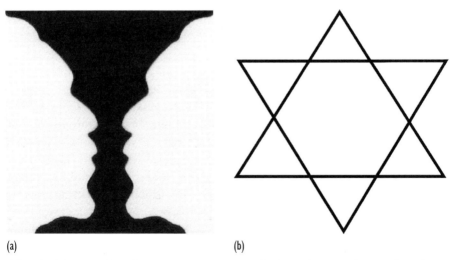

(a)                              (b)

**1.2** (a) Ambiguity: vase or faces? (b) Emergence: two overlapping triangles also contain emergent features such as a hexagon and a six-pointed star.

talent, as a leading member of the structural design team for some of the most challenging buildings in the world, such as the Sydney Opera House and the Pompidou Centre in Paris, and in his own engineering design work in light-weight structures. The uncertainty of design is both the frustration and the joy that designers get from their activity; they have learned to live with the fact that design proposals may remain ambiguous and uncertain until quite late in the process. Designers will generate early tentative solutions, but also leave many options open for as long as possible; they are prepared to regard solution concepts as temporarily imprecise and often inconclusive.

Another common theme from Davies's interviews is that designers need to use sketches, drawings and models of all kinds as a way of exploring problem and solution together, and of making some progress when faced with the complexity of design. For example, Jack Howe said that, when uncertain how to proceed, 'I draw something. Even if it's "potty" I draw it. The act of drawing seems to clarify my thoughts.' He means that, when faced with a blank sheet of paper, he can at least draw something that may at first seem silly or inappropriate, but which provides a starting point to which he can respond; if it doesn't seem right, why doesn't it? Designing, it seems, is difficult to conduct by purely internal mental processes; the designer needs to interact with an external representation. The activity of sketching, drawing or modelling provides some of the circumstances by which a designer puts him- or herself into the design situation and engages with the exploration of both the problem and its solution. There is a cognitive limit to the amount of complexity that can be handled internally; sketching provides a temporary, external store for tentative ideas, and supports the 'dialogue' that the designer has between problem and solution.

Summarising from the interviews with RDIs, Robert Davies and Reg Talbot also identified some personality characteristics which seem key to making these people successful in dealing constructively with uncertainty, and the risks and opportunities that present themselves in the process of designing. 'One of the characteristics of these people,' they suggested, 'is that they are very open to all kinds of experience, particularly influences relevant to their design problem. Their awareness is high. They are sensitive to nuances in their internal and external environments. They are ready, in many ways, to notice particular coincidences in the rhythm of events which other people, because they are less aware and less open to their experience, fail to notice. These designers are able to recognise opportunities in the way coincidences offer prospects and risks for attaining some desirable goal or grand scheme of things. They identify favourable conjectures and become deeply involved, applying their utmost efforts, sometimes "quite forgetting" other people and/ or things only peripherally involved ... What turns an event from a crisis into an opportunity, it seems, depends upon the way events are construed by the individual rather than the nature of the events per se.' Successful designers are optimists, exploring hopefully, dedicated to the task in hand. And, like all good explorers, they are opportunists, taking advantage of any unexpected openings or vantage points, and spotting what look like fruitful ways ahead.

Many aspects of design ability that emerge from Davies's study are also reflected in another set of interviews with highly successful designers, conducted by Bryan Lawson, who interviewed a number of internationally leading architects. The importance of drawing and sketching within the design process is one thing especially emphasised by these architects. For example, the British architect Richard MacCormac said, 'Whenever we have a design session or a crit review session in the office I cannot say anything until I've got a pencil in my hand ... I feel the pencil to be my spokesman, as it were ... I haven't got an imagination that can tell me what I've got without drawing it ... I use drawing as a process of criticism and discovery.' Here, MacCormac is saying that he uses drawing both as a means of imaging, imagining or discovering something that he cannot construct just in his mind, and as a means of communicating with others – the pencil is his 'spokesman', communicating by means of what he draws. Note that the 'spokesman' is both critic and discoverer, which reinforces just how cognitively important the act of sketching is to the designer. And note also that he and his colleagues in his office must be able to read, as well as 'write', substantial and significant information from sketches and drawings.

The Spanish engineer-architect Santiago Calatrava also uses sketching and drawing as a key part of his design process. Lawson reported that Calatrava is 'a prolific drawer, but one senses that his graphical output is never the result of a wish to produce a drawing but rather to understand a problem. He seldom works at a drawing table but usually on rather small pads of paper perhaps at about A3 size. "I could take a big piece of paper and draw the whole thing, but I prefer to concentrate." His design process depends heavily on a stream of graphical output, sometimes pencil sketches, often watercolours, which he uses to communicate his ideas to his staff. He sees this very much as a journey of exploration with each sketch following on from its predecessors as the ideas develop. "You are discovering the layers of your project ... I mean, to start with you see the thing in your mind and it doesn't exist on paper and then you start making simple sketches and organising things and then you start doing layer after layer ... it is very much a dialogue." He likes to have pads or books of paper in front of him so he can see how far he has got down this journey'. Although Calatrava says here that, unlike MacCormac, he can 'see the thing in his mind', it is clear that what he may initially 'see' has to be 'concentrated upon' in an external representation. The early design concept has to be developed and explored through the 'dialogue' of sketching, through a related visual and cognitive process, like MacCormac's, of criticism and discovery.

Also as in the study by Davies, Lawson identified from his interviews something of the complex relationship in design between problem and solution. Richard MacCormac spoke of defining the problem through attempting solutions: 'Issues which are the stuff of the thing often only come out when you try and produce a scheme, and therefore the design process defines objectives in a way in which the brief could never do.' In fact, when I had interviewed Richard MacCormac, some years before Lawson's study, he told me: 'I don't think you can design anything just by absorbing information and then hoping to synthesise it into a solution. What you need to know about the problem only becomes apparent as you're trying to solve it.' This confirms a view that the design brief is not a specification for a solution, but the starting point for an exploration. Like Denys Lasdun saying that the architect's job is to give the client something other than 'what he wants', Richard MacCormac told Lawson, 'Often in competitions the winning scheme is the one that tells the client something that they never knew before … something that is terribly important to them and was not in the brief.' This is the reason why unsuccessful design competition entrants sometimes complain that the winner 'didn't stick to the brief'. As Lawson commented, 'Although we tend to admire designers for their solutions, it is often their ability to find the right problems which distinguishes good from adequate or poor design.'

Lawson also suggested that good designers are good at coping with uncertainty. Several of his interviewed architects spoke of carrying on 'parallel processes' of cognition relevant to the same design job at the same time. For example, the Czech architect Eva Jiricna spoke of working on detail junctions of materials at the same time as on general spatial concepts of a design. Lawson found a strong example of what he called such 'parallel lines of thought' in the American architect Robert Venturi's description of working on his design for the Sainsbury Wing extension to the National Gallery in London. One particular line of thought concerned ideas for relating the circulation system in the new building to that in the older part (issues of the plan, and of floor levels), while another was for relating together the external appearances of the new and old parts (issues of the elevation, and of architectural styles). Lawson suggests that Venturi kept these two sets of ideas in progress, both equally important to his design thinking, before resolving them into a single solution. 'The problem for the designer,' Lawson commented, 'is when the attempt should be made to reconcile all the ideas, or lines of thought, which are developing. If this is attempted too early, ideas which are still poorly understood may get lost, while if this is left too late they may become fossilised and too rigid. There is no formula or easy answer to this conundrum, the resolution of which probably depends almost entirely on the skill and sensitivity of the designer. However, what seems clear is that a degree of bravery is required to allow these lines of thought to remain parallel rather longer than might seem reasonable to the inexperienced designer.' Coping with uncertainty, as Ted Happold emphasised, seems to be a key factor in design ability.

One way to cope with uncertainty is to try to impose order. Jane Darke also interviewed a number of successful architects, and noticed how they sought to impose order on the rather nebulous problems they faced. Some brought to the problem a personal set of guiding principles that offered starting points, some sought to find starting points in the particularities of the site on which they were to build. In each case, Darke observed how these starting points enabled the designers to limit the problem to something manageable, to provide a narrower focus within which they could work. 'The greatest variety reduction or narrowing down of the range of solutions occurs early on in the design process,' she observed, 'with a conjecture or conceptualisation of a possible solution. Further understanding of the problem is gained by testing this conjectured solution.' The designers imposed a limited set of objectives, or an idea about the building form, as a 'primary generator', as Darke called it, a means of instantiating a solution concept. This seems to be a necessary part of the design process, because a solution concept cannot be derived directly from the problem statement; the designer has to bring something to it.

## Deconstructing what Designers Do

What designers say about what they do can of course be rather biased, or based on partial recall, or limited by their willingness or ability to articulate what are, after all, complex cognitive activities. But I said before that it is possible to unravel even Philippe Starck's mystical account of the conception of his *Juicy Salif* lemon squeezer into a much less mysterious explanation. To do this, I am drawing upon an exercise in deconstructing this particular design act by Peter Lloyd and Dirk Snelders, in which they utilised what Philippe Starck has said about himself in various interviews, what (little) he has said about the conception of the lemon squeezer, and the evidence of Starck's very first design sketches for it.

In the late 1980s, Philippe Starck was already a renowned designer of a wide range of different products. The Alessi company had started a new series of products designed by internationally famous designers, including kettles and coffee pots by architects Michael Graves and Aldo Rossi, and cutlery and condiment sets by industrial designers Richard Sapper and Ettore Sottsass. Alessi invited Starck to offer a new product in the 'designer' series, a lemon squeezer. Starck went to Italy to visit Alessi and discuss the project. He then took a short break on the small island of Capraia, just off the Tuscan coast, and went to dine in a pizzeria restaurant, Il Corsaro. He was obviously already thinking about the lemon squeezer project, because, as he waited for his food, he began to sketch on the paper place mat. At first, the sketches were just very rough images of a fairly conventional form of lemon squeezer (see the centre-right area of the place mat, Figure 1.3), but then something happened to inspire a leap to making sketches of something quite different – his anti-pasto plate of baby squid had arrived, and Starck began to get his 'vision of a squid-like lemon squeezer'! His sketches on the place mat now became images of strange forms with big bodies and long legs, and eventually (bottom left in Figure 1.3) something emerged that is now recognisable as the *Juicy Salif* concept.

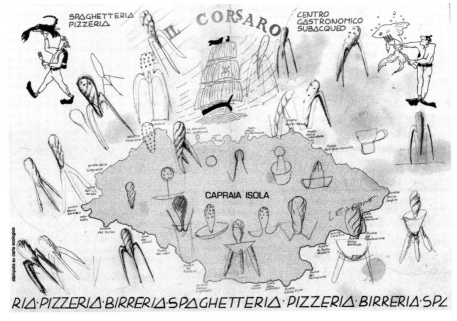

**1.3** Starck's design sketches for the lemon squeezer on the restaurant placemat.

Lloyd and Snelders recount what probably went on in this quick process of creative sketching and thinking, as Starck drew for inspiration not only on the squid but also on his boyhood interests in sci-fi comics and space-ship imagery. 'First he tries to make a conventional lemon squeezer out of a squid, but then he realises that won't really work. The squid begins to evolve – Philippe has always been interested in evolution – into something with legs, but he doesn't like it. It seems to be dragging, injured almost.' Here, one might interject, Starck seems to be using his pencil, like Richard MacCormac, in a process of discovery and invention. 'He keeps going, eating while he sketches. His sketches abstractly remind him of the old comics he used to read … Things begin to gel in his mind, and from the dragging creature emerges a lighter, three-legged form. Like one of the spaceships he used to think about jetting up to space in. He likes the form, it's "working" … The next morning he phones Alessi, "I've got a lemon squeezer for you," he teases. Of course there are a few details to work out, exact dimensions, what material to use, how to get the juice out of the lemon efficiently. But these are all sub-problems; someone else can solve them. The main problem is solved.'

So we see that the concept for the strange new type of lemon squeezer did not leap fully formed into Philippe Starck's mind, but emerged, albeit pretty quickly, in a process of sketching inspired by seeing a squid shape as a potential source of form, and driven by recall of other imagery. This other imagery comes from Starck's repertoire of other interests, including aircraft design (his father's occupation), space rockets, science fiction, comic strips, and organic evolution. Lloyd and Snelders suggest that Starck has retained a kind of juvenile enthusiasm for futuristic imagery. The lemon squeezer will be made of aluminium. 'Aluminium as a material has been said to give a feeling of "nostalgia for the future",' say Lloyd and Snelders, 'and there are other features of the lemon squeezer that one can associate with a future imagined from the past. Chief among these is its rocket or spaceship associa-tions. Not with rockets of the present, but with old-style rockets, like those of Soviet inventors. At the time rockets promised an exciting, high-tech future of space exploration, a long way from war-torn planet Earth. This "future of the past" feeling is maintained by the streamlining of the squeezer's body (a teardrop being a good aerodynamic shape). Starting in the [nineteen-] thirties and continuing into the fifties streamlining made everything look modern, and the metaphor of streamlining, speeding unhindered towards the future, became a metaphor of social and technological progress. In the late 1980s streamlining might just be thought of as retro, but it could also be taken as ironic, especially as there *is* actually a fluid moving over the surface of the lemon squeezer, albeit not at a speed that streamlining would help at all.'

In deconstructing Philippe Starck's creative act, Lloyd and Snelders implied that the 'squid-like' concept was not an inexplicable flash of inspiration from nowhere, but that it arose rather more prosaically by applying an analogy (the form of the squid) to the problem that was in Starck's mind (a novel form for a lemon squeezer). This kind of analogy-making is often proposed as a means of encouraging creative thinking. What was particularly striking in this case was Starck's ability to make such a leap of imagination from 'squid' to 'lemon squeezer'. Thereafter, Lloyd and Snelders suggested, Starck, in developing the concept, was doing what many designers do, which is to draw upon a repertoire of precedents, of remembered images and recollections of other objects that helped him to give a more coherent, practicable and attractive form to the concept.

## Watching what Designers Do

A more direct form of enquiry into understanding what designers do is actually to watch them at work, observing their activities. Such studies not only report on what was observed to happen, but also try to add another layer of explanation of the nature of designing. Larry Bucciarelli made a series of extensive, very detailed, participant-observer studies of engineering design projects in three different companies. Large projects demand an important aspect of design ability, that of reconciling the variety of interests – technical, financial, social, aesthetic, etc. – that inevitably have to coalesce around a major project. In these cases, designing becomes not just a personal, cognitive process, but a shared, social process. The main conclusion that Bucciarelli stressed is how even engineering design, traditionally seen as a strictly technical process, is in reality a social process of interaction and negotiation between the different participants who each bring to bear their own 'object world' – their own specific knowledge and awareness of aspects of the object being designed. His thesis is that 'the process of designing is a process of achieving consensus among participants with different "interests" in the design, and that those different interests are not reconcilable in object-world terms … The process is necessarily social and requires the participants to negotiate their differences and construct meaning through direct, and preferably face-to-face, exchange.' The social nature of designing, he suggested, results in acknowledging the inevitability of uncertainty and ambiguity, even within the process of engineering design. 'Ambiguity is essential to design process, allowing participants the freedom to manoeuvre independently within object worlds and providing room for the recasting of meaning in the negotiations with others.'

Bucciarelli took an ethnographic approach to studying design activity, by participating in the normal, day-to-day activities of the engineers. In another ethnographic study, of graphic designers, Dianne Murray also recorded the social nature of design in practice, and emphasised the openness and shared activities of a design studio: 'Briefing sessions take place in the studio in clear sight and sound of everyone. Work in progress is left on drawing boards; discarded sketches, photocopies, printouts and transparencies are left lying around on desks or on the light box … Design is not hidden, it is constructed in public so other people can read it, and accepting commentary on it from somebody else is part of a tradition they embody.' From close-up studies such as these by Bucciarelli and Murray, common features of design thinking and working emerge from quite different fields of design practice.

Peter Rowe made a set of case study observations of architectural design. These studies were of major buildings set in large American cities, designed by leading architects. Rowe noticed in all three studies that the architects' attention switched regularly between solution concepts and problem exploration – between developing ideas for building form and investigating the implications of those ideas in terms of the design brief and technical feasibility. He characterised the progress of the design activity as 'episodic', or as a kind of 'series of related skirmishes with various aspects of the problem at hand'. This episodic structure was manifest in a number of ways: 'First, there is the "to and fro" movement between areas of concern ... a movement back and forth between exploration of architectural form and evaluation of programme, structure, and other technical issues. Second, there seem to be periods of unfettered speculation, followed by more sober and contemplative episodes during which the designer "takes stock of the situation". Third, each episode seems to have a particular orientation that preoccupies the designer. We might say that the organising principles involved in each episode take on a life of their own, as the designer becomes absorbed in exploring the possibilities that they promise.'

This sounds like the typically 'exploratory' approach of the designer – seeking opportunities that offer ways to progress, pushing ahead along promising avenues, and pausing from time to time to evaluate what has been achieved so far. But Rowe made a criticism of this way of proceeding; it seemed to him to be unnecessarily chancy, and inefficient. 'These episodes', he commented, 'such as the various massing exercises with building volumes, often became very speculative as the designer "pressed on", as it were, when information from another quarter might have resolved the problem at hand more economically. Such situations often subsequently gave rise to a certain amount of backtracking, as the designer retrenched to what seemed a more advantageous position.' It is as though the designer adopts a blinkered approach, overly focused on a particular solution concept, and doggedly 'pressing on' when a more considered and reflective approach, and consideration of alternative solution concepts, might save time and effort in the long run.

The issue here seems to be to do with the predominance of the 'primary generator' in restricting the designer's thought patterns. There is a 'dominant influence', Rowe suggested, 'exerted by initial design ideas on subsequent problem-solving directions'. Of course, he acknowledged, 'designers inevitably bring certain organising principles to a problem at the outset'. But there is a danger in clinging to these ideas, a danger of failing to see their inadequacies:

'Even when severe problems are encountered, a considerable effort is made to make the initial idea work, rather than to stand back and adopt a fresh point of departure.' This seems to be a weakness in the designer's attitude and approach – investing too much effort into early, perhaps inadequate, ideas of a solution concept; even perhaps being too attached to a 'favourite' idea, rather than being more objective, more concerned to generate and evaluate a range of options.

Why should experienced designers behave in this apparently limited way? A clue lies in an analysis of cases of urban design similar to those studied by Rowe. Peter Levin also found that designers jumped to ideas for solutions (or partial solutions) before they had fully formulated the problem. We know that early solution conjectures offer a way to proceed with ill-defined problems. Levin suggested that, in order to generate these conjectures, some information, or 'missing ingredient', has to be provided by the designer himself. 'The designer knows (consciously or unconsciously) that some ingredient must be added to the information that he already has in order to arrive at a unique solution. This knowledge is in itself not enough in design problems, of course. He has to look for the extra ingredient, and he uses powers of conjecture and original thought to do so.' Levin suggested that this extra ingredient is often an 'ordering principle' and hence we find the formal properties that are so often evident in designers' work, from towns designed as rectangular grids to teacups designed as regular cylinders. This is the same sort of thing as Rowe saw, such as 'the various massing exercises with building volumes', in which the designer seeks an 'ordering principle' around which a solution concept can be structured. It could be that designers have to invest some significant cognitive effort in generating these concepts, and so they are reluctant to let go of them.

The most influential study of a designer at work has been that by Donald Schön. The influence of the study is largely due to its being set within Schön's broader series of studies of professional practice (ranging from psychotherapy to management) that he used to establish his theory of reflective practice, or 'how professionals think in action'. The study has also been influential because Schön's analysis of what he observed is acute and sensitive; both designers and design researchers (those with personal design experience) recognise the veracity of the analysis. What is surprising is that such an influential study is based on just one, partial example of design activity – and even that is not a 'real' design example, but is taken from observing an experienced designer tutoring a student in a university architectural design studio.

Schön established his theory of reflective practice as a counter to the prevailing theory of technical rationality, or the constrained application of scientific theory and technique to practical problems. He was seeking a new 'epistemology of practice' that would help explain and account for how competent practitioners actually engage with their practice – a 'kind of knowing', he argued, that is different from the knowledge found in textbooks. In his analysis of the case studies that provided the foundations for his theory, he began with the assumption that 'competent practitioners usually know more than they can say. They exhibit a kind of knowing-in-practice, most of which is tacit.' He identified a cognitive process of reflection-in-action as the intelligence that guides 'intuitive' behaviour in practical contexts of thinking-and-acting – something like 'thinking on your feet'. At the heart of reflection-in-action is the 'frame experiment' in which the practitioner frames, or poses a way of seeing the problematic situation at hand.

According to Schön, designing proceeds as 'a reflective conversation with the situation,' an interactive process based on posing a problem frame and exploring its implications in 'moves' that investigate the arising solution possibilities. A designer, he argued, is faced with a situation of complexity. 'Because of this complexity, the designer's moves tend, happily or unhappily, to produce consequences other than those intended. When this happens, the designer may take account of the unintended changes he has made in the situation by forming new appreciations and understandings and by making new moves. He shapes the situation, in accordance with his initial appreciation of it, the situation "talks back", and he responds to the situation's back-talk.'

The design example that Schön uses is that of a tutor, 'Quist', helping a student, 'Petra', with her problem of designing a school on a sloping site. Because Quist has to explain his own thinking to Petra, his words, and the sketches he makes at the same time, give an insight into his cognitive processes, his reflection-in-action. The talking (i.e. the thinking) and the drawing go on in parallel, as other designers have said.

Petra is 'stuck' in the early part of her design process: she has drawn a series of connected, L-shaped classroom blocks, but she has a problem fitting them to the site. 'I've tried to butt the shape of the building into the contours of the land there – but the shape doesn't fit into the slope,' she explains. Quist suggests that she stops trying to work so closely to the site's contours, and instead that she should seek to impose her building geometry onto the site. 'You should begin with a discipline,' he says, 'even if it is arbitrary … you can always break it open later.' Quist starts to sketch in plan and section, exploring the implications of the 'discipline' of form that he is now imposing on the site. As he explores, he begins to find some of those 'new appreciations and understandings' in the design. With his more aggressive approach to the site, he sees how, in section, 'We get a total differential potential here from one end of the classroom to the far end of the other. There is fifteen feet max, right – so we could have as much as five-foot intervals, which for a kid is maximum height, right? The section through here could be one of nooks in here and the differentiation between this unit and this would be at two levels.' The idea of 'kid-height nooks' is something that Quist discovers as a potential in his solution concept, not something that was in the design brief; it is an emergent property of his designing. In Schön's terms, it is an 'unintended change' in the situation, which Quist interprets as a positive indicator of the appropriateness of the problem frame that he has set up. A little later, as he continues designing, other positive aspects are spotted and reinforced in the emerging design – and even the qualities of the site come back into play, as here: 'Then you might carry the gallery level through – and look down into here – which is nice. Let the land generate some sub-ideas here, which could be very nice. Maybe the cafeteria needn't be such a formal function – maybe it could come into here to get summer sun here and winter here.'

One thing Quist demonstrates is that he has the confidence to ask 'what if?' What if we carve the L-shaped blocks more deeply into the site? What if we work with a system of five-feet height intervals? What if we create a gallery-level circulation space? These 'what if' conjectures are the 'moves' that

Schön identified: 'Each has implications binding on later moves. And each creates new problems to be described and solved. Quist designs by spinning out a web of moves, consequences, implications, appreciations, and further moves ... Each move is a local experiment which contributes to the global experiment of reframing the problem ... As Quist reflects on the unexpected consequences and implications of his moves, he listens to the situation's back-talk, forming new appreciations which guide his further moves.'

As designing proceeds, the sketches become a record of the moves and their implications. Many things remain tentative, but some are selected as positive outcomes of the 'what if?' conjectures, and are given temporary identities as features to be retained. Schön suggested that these are choice-points within the process. 'As he reflects-in-action on the situation created by his earlier moves, the designer must consider not only the present choice but the tree of further choices to which it leads, each of which has different meanings in relation to the systems of implications set up by earlier moves. Quist's virtuosity lies in his ability to string out design webs of great complexity. But even he cannot hold in mind an indefinitely expanding web. At some point, he must move from a "what if?" to a decision which then becomes a design node with binding implications for further moves. Thus there is a continually evolving system of implications within which the designer reflects-in-action.'

What we gain from Schön's analysis is a clear account of a typical, fast-moving, 'thinking on your feet', live example of designing. The initial problematic situation is 'framed' by the designer. Quist's framing adopts the given of Petra's starting point of a series of linked L-shaped blocks (he is tutoring her in how to develop her solution idea, not starting from scratch with his own idea) and poses the implicit question, 'How can we make these blocks fit into the sloping site in a coherent way?' He works through a series of thinking-actions of moving-seeing-moving; that is, of posing a 'what if?' move, looking at what results (in his sketches), reflecting on the consequences (good or bad), and making another, related move. One move leads to another, through the medium of the sketches, which not only record the process of moves but also provoke thoughts and initiate new moves.

Something similar must have been happening in Rowe's studies of architectural design, even though the design projects were on a much larger scale. The designers spin out a complex web of inter-related moves, reflections, decisions, and further moves. They invest a great deal of cognitive effort in spinning and maintaining these webs, and so perhaps it is no wonder that they are reluctant to 'stand back and adopt a fresh point of departure'. But sometimes it is necessary; a problem frame can prove to be inappropriate, or the designer lacks the ability to maintain a positive sequence of moves within the frame, and so a new departure point, a new problem frame becomes necessary.

An aspect of Schön's study that helps to make it particularly informative is that it is based on the 'live' data of Quist's talking and drawing. Because he is tutoring, Quist externalises his thinking for the benefit of the student, when normally it would be a silent, internal cognitive process. This therefore provides an example of something like a 'think aloud' protocol study, of the type which has come to be used extensively to investigate how designers think. The 'protocols' are the sequence of thoughts, reflected in the comments made by the designer. These protocol studies are normally conducted as a laboratory type of study, in which a designer is asked to 'think aloud' as he or she works through a short design project. Detailed evidence from these kinds of study will be used frequently in the later chapters of this book.

These various studies of design in action, based on watching what designers do, have tended to confirm what designers say about the nature of designing. There is the need to tolerate and work with uncertainty, to have the confidence to conjecture and to explore, to interact constructively with sketches and models, and to rely upon one's 'intuitive' powers of reflection-in-action.

## Thinking about what Designers Do

The criticisms that Peter Rowe made of the way that designers tended to cling for too long to solution conjectures that were proving inadequate have also been reflected in comments by others. This and other early criticisms of the typical ways that designers work led to attempts to provide design methods or guidelines that would encourage designers to work more 'rationally'. Such guidelines generally outline a systematic procedure of first analysing the problem as fully as possible, then breaking this into sub-problems, finding suitable sub-solutions, evaluating these and then selecting and combining them into an overall solution. It is basically a process of analysis-synthesis-evaluation. However, this kind of procedure has been criticised in the design world because it seems to be based on inappropriate models imported from theories of problem solving and 'rational behaviour', and therefore runs counter to designers' more 'intuitive' ways of thinking and reasoning.

Several theoretical arguments have been advanced in support of the view that design reasoning is different from the conventionally acknowledged forms of inductive and deductive reasoning. For example, Lionel March distinguished design's mode of reasoning from those of logic and science. He pointed out that 'Logic has interests in abstract forms. Science investigates extant forms. Design initiates novel forms. A scientific hypothesis is not the same thing as a design hypothesis. A logical proposition is not to be mistaken for a design proposal. A speculative design cannot be determined logically, because the mode of reasoning involved is essentially abductive.'

March argued that the two conventionally understood forms of reasoning – deductive and inductive – only apply logically to analytical and evaluative types of activity. But the type of activity that is most particularly associated with design is that of synthesis, for which there is no commonly acknowledged form of reasoning. March drew on the work of the philosopher C. S. Peirce to identify this missing concept of 'abductive' reasoning. According to Peirce, 'Deduction proves that something *must* be; induction shows that something *actually* is operative; abduction suggests that something *may* be.' It is this hypothesising of what *may* be, the act of producing proposals or conjectures, that is central to designing.

Deductive reasoning is the reasoning of formal logic: if $a$ is the same as $b$, and $b$ is the same as $c$, then $a$ is the same as $c$. Inductive reasoning is the logic of science: you observe all the swans in a given region; you note that each and every swan is white; you form the rule that 'all swans are white' (which you may find is false when you move to another region and discover some black swans). Abduction is the logic of design: you are asked to design a telephone for mature people; you know that mature people like clarity and elegant forms and colours; you propose a design with a smoothly contoured, soft-white case and clear, black buttons (one of many possible proposals for achieving clarity and elegance).

Instead of 'abductive' reasoning, Lionel March preferred to call designing 'productive reasoning' because the designer has to produce a composition, or product. 'Appositional reasoning' also seems to be a suitable term to use, because the designer makes a proposal for a solution that, when juxtaposed to the problem, seems to be an apposite response. Unlike conventional logic, a design solution cannot be derived directly from the problem, but can only be matched to it. Unlike the scientist, who searches for many cases to substantiate a rule, and then one case to falsify it, the designer can be gratified in being able to produce just one satisfactory case that gives an appropriate result.

A comprehensive analysis of why the classic methods of reasoning in problem solving are inappropriate in design has been provided by Henrik Gedenryd. Working from a cognitive science perspective, and applying it especially in the context of interaction design, Gedenryd argued against the view of cognition as a purely rational, 'intra-mental' (i.e. solely within the mind) activity, and in favour of recognising it as a practical, interactive activity. He concluded that 'the mind working on its own is only a circumscribed portion of the full cognitive system'; the full system comprises mind, action and world, or a combination of thinking and acting within a physical environment. The designer's natural way of working encompasses that larger system through interacting with temporary models of the situation being designed for. The range of design techniques such as sketching, prototyping, mockups, scenarios, etc., enable the designer to make 'an inquiry into the future situation of use'. These techniques 'make the world a part of cognition', and provide the designer with a set of 'situating strategies'. Hence, Gedenryd provided a theoretical understanding for the important role of these techniques and strategies in design. He showed that abstract thought alone cannot satisfactorily perform the complex task of designing.

## The Natural Intelligence of Design

The most significant outcome from the varied studies and research into design practice has been the growth of respect for the inherent, natural intelligence that is manifested in design ability. Early attempts to reshape the process of design into something more rational and systematic were founded perhaps on a disrespect for this natural design ability, and a strong desire to impose order onto design thinking. There was a desire to recast design almost as a form of science, and to replace conventional design activities with completely new ones, based on technical rationality.

These original aims may well have been an understandable reaction to a previous view of design ability as an ineffable, mysterious art. There are still those who regard design thinking as ineffable, and there are still those whose lack of understanding of design ability still leads them into attempts to reformulate design activities in inappropriate ways. However, at the core of the discipline of design there is now a more mature, informed and enlightened view of design ability. This mature view has grown from a better, research-based understanding of the nature of design ability, from analysis of its strengths and weaknesses, and from a desire to defend and nurture that ability.

As we have seen, one way of studying design thinking that has helped particularly to develop that better understanding has been through case studies of designers at work. The next part of this book begins a series of case studies of designers and design activity that will occur throughout the book. The case studies are intended to provide resources for the study of high-quality design thinking, with information and data drawn from both interviews and experimental investigations. In the next two chapters we will study two outstanding designers, with the chapters based on my own interviews and conversations with the designers.

## Sources

Full references are included in the Bibliography.

Larry Bucciarelli: *Designing Engineers*.
Jane Darke: The primary generator and the design process, *Design Studies*.
Robert Davies: *A Psychological Enquiry into the Origination and Implementation of Ideas*.
Robert Davies and Reg Talbot: Experiencing ideas, *Design Studies*.
Henrik Gedenryd: *How Designers Work*.
Bryan Lawson: *Design In Mind*.
Peter Levin: *Decision Making in Urban Design*.
Peter Lloyd and Dirk Snelders: What was Philippe Starck thinking of? *Design Studies*.
Lionel March: The Logic of Design, in *The Architecture of Form*.
Dianne Murray: An Ethnographic Study of Graphic Designers, in *European Conference on Computer Supported Cooperative Work*.
Peter Rowe: *Design Thinking*.
Donald Schön: *The Reflective Practitioner*.

# 2

# Designing to Win

Our first case study is of an outstanding designer who has had a long and distinguished record as a highly successful and highly innovative designer in a highly competitive environment, that of Formula One racing car design. As a young graduate engineer, Gordon Murray moved to Britain from his home in South Africa where he had built and raced his own car in club events. He joined the Brabham Formula One racing car team as a designer-draughtsman, and quite soon was appointed chief designer. For twelve years, he carried the major responsibility for the design of a series of innovative and frequently successful racing cars. Brabham cars designed by him were driven by Nelson Piquet to win the World Championship in 1981 and 1983. In 1987, Gordon Murray moved to the McLaren Formula One team as technical director. Through all four race seasons from 1988 to 1991, McLaren cars designed by Murray and his team, driven by Alain Prost and Ayrton Senna, won both the

Drivers' Championship and the Constructors' Championship. In all, Gordon Murray's cars won 51 Grand Prix races.

Gordon Murray then became technical director of McLaren Cars Limited, an offshoot of the Formula One team, and became responsible for the design and development of a completely new, road-going 'super car' – the McLaren F1 (Figure 2.1), which attracted immense attention as the 'ultimate' sports car. As well as many technical innovations, the F1 featured a novel seating arrangement, with the driver positioned centrally and two passenger seats beside but slightly behind the driver, in an 'arrowhead' configuration (Figure 2.2).

**2.1** The McLaren F1.

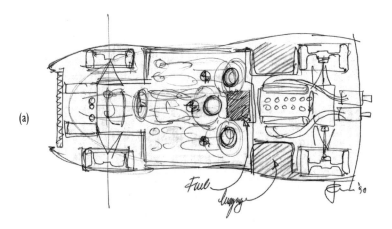

(a)

(b)

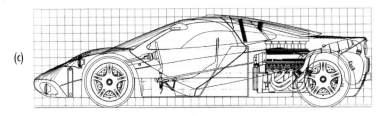

(c)

**2.2** (a) Gordon Murray's sketch for the McLaren F1, showing the three-person seating arrangement with passengers slightly behind the central driver; (b) overhead view of the McLaren F1; (c) detail drawing side/cutaway-view of the McLaren F1.

The F1 was designed on the same rigorous principles as a Formula One car. These principles were proved when GTR versions of the F1 were produced for competition in sports car races; at their first outing, the 1995 Le Mans 24-hours race, McLaren F1s came first, third, fourth and fifth. Gordon Murray went on to design another super car, the Mercedes McLaren SLR, and then took a radical change of direction into the design of a small, cheap city-car, the T.25, first announced in 2008, and then as the T.27 electric-powered version in 2009.

## Formula One Designing

Formula One racing car design is, of course, significantly different from almost every other kind of design domain. Gordon Murray likens it to war. Although he has never been in a war, engineering and technological development in wartime is the closest analogy to Formula One he can think of, with resources – human, financial and technical – being poured into the design and construction of machines that must have, and maintain, a vital performance edge over those of the 'enemy'. Throughout the nine-month Formula One season there is a battle to be fought on a different field every two weeks, with a new campaign starting again every year.

This constant war-like atmosphere creates tremendous pressure, particularly on someone in the position Gordon Murray was in for many years with Brabham of being totally in control of, and responsible for, the complete technical operation: designing, constructing, testing, racing and organising, throughout the year, and from one year to the next. With the calendar of Grand Prix races fixed in advance, there is also constant time pressure, with no possibility allowed of missing a single race or practice session.

There are also, of course, the 'rules of engagement' for this perpetual 'war': the Formula One technical and sporting regulations, which minutely and precisely specify the physical and operational limits within which the teams must compete. Gordon Murray regards the regulations (the constraints, or design specification) of racing car design, along with its intense pressure and competition, as fundamental to the necessity to innovate. With every team working within the same constraints, only innovation, coupled with constant refinement and improvement, can provide the competitive edge. In other design fields, as he has discovered, the lack of regulations can be slightly bewildering, allowing the designer to wander at whim in a very loosely bounded solution space. Although he has tried working in other design fields, Gordon Murray seems to find them uncomfortable. Outside of racing car design he thinks that there just is not enough pressure on the designer, nor tight enough regulations, nor strong enough competition, for radical, innovative design thinking.

Many other designers might suggest that the one significant constraint they have to design within, which Formula One designers do not have, is that of money – the financial limit on what their product can cost. But Gordon Murray does not entirely agree. He claims that at Brabham the budgets were relatively small for Formula One, perhaps only one-third of the budgets of bigger teams, but that did not limit their innovation potential. A relative shortage of money meant the Brabham team might do less testing, or carry fewer spares, but that did not stop innovation which, he claims, comes down to people and their environment. 'It comes from the environment and the situation you're in; you're governed by these regulations; you're in this sort of a war situation, you've got a battle every two weeks; and you're desperate to try and think of things all the time – alongside all the normal design [improvement] processes which are more laborious … I can't tell you how hyper it is, relative to architecture, bridge design, furniture design …' And as we will see later, in his city-car design he applied his same principles of design thinking within a context of saving every penny of cost.

## Radical Innovations

Throughout a racing season there is constant work to make continuous improvements and adjustments to the current car design. These may be responses to obvious shortcomings such as component failures, or to the drivers' comments about the car's performance and handling, either in general or in relation to certain corners or features of certain race circuits. The performance improvements aimed for may seem incredibly tiny by other standards – perhaps one-tenth of a second on a lap – but they can make the difference between being first or second in the race. And at the same time, every other team is also making constant improvements, so the situation is never static.

This creates constant, relentless pressure on the designer to keep making design improvements. But there is a limit to what can be achieved with any car design, before a jump has to be made to basically a new design, an innovation. As Gordon says, 'Given the situation and the pressure at any one time, you do get to the brick wall. I mean, you're doing all these normal modifications, you know you can't go any quicker, you need to make the step forward.' Typically, such a step forward happens during the short close-season, when every team seeks to start the coming new season with an advantage over its rivals.

The constant pressure during the racing season breeds a fervour to succeed that never stops, Gordon says: 'You gotta go quicker, gotta go quicker.' The pressure then to come up with something new becomes intense, and the responsibility is all yours, 'and you get more and more sort of – panicky, almost'.

The situation can only be resolved by a new car design. In many instances, and for most teams, this will be a new version of the previous season's car; perhaps a new chassis, new suspension, or new engine to be accommodated; perhaps a change in regulations to be met. For Gordon Murray it would often mean trying a 'step forward', a radical new concept. In the midst of the pressure, the fervour, the panic, he 'used to get breakthroughs, I mean I used to get like suddenly a mental block's lifted'. These breakthroughs would come as a sudden illumination: 'I know it's a cliché, but I did have a lot of good ideas in the bath, I really did.' The illuminations came, again in classical form, after long periods of preoccupation with the problem, and after what Gordon Murray emphasises as the most important factor in innovative design, of reconsidering the problem situation from first principles; he stresses the need to 'keep looking back at fundamental physical principles'.

Another crucial factor is the motivation to carry the bright idea through into detailed implementation. Again, intense pressure, even in the brief close-season, ensures that ideas that look certain to be winners will be pushed through to detailed implementation with the same fervour as in the racing season. Other possibly good ideas are discarded on a rapid evaluation of their implications for a car's weight, performance or handling. In racing car design, it is not just a matter of having ideas, but of really implementing ideas that are going to improve performance, of having to 'do it', as Gordon says; 'You have the idea, but you have to do it, and that's what cuts the bullshit out.'

## Hydro-pneumatic Suspension

As one example of radical innovation, Gordon Murray refers to the development at Brabham of a hydro-pneumatic suspension system. In the early 1980s, the Formula One governing body, FISA, became concerned to reduce the 'ground effect' on racing cars. This effect had been pioneered on the Lotus team's cars; smooth underbodies lying very close to the ground, side skirts and careful aerodynamic design provided a ground-effect downforce which increased the car's grip on the track surface. This meant much higher cornering speeds were possible, until some people were worried about the heavy g-force effects that were being imposed on the drivers that might cause them to lose consciousness. FISA decided to ban 'sliding' skirts, but allowed fixed skirts and set a minimum underbody ground clearance of 6 cm. For Gordon Murray this sudden change in regulations was a stimulus to innovation.

What turned out to be his first World Championship-winning car 'came absolutely from the regulation change. You sit there and you read the regulations and think, how we are going to do it? How the hell can we get ground effect back? What [the regulations] said was "At all times the car will have a 6cm gap between the bodywork and the ground … and there can be no driver-operated device to change that gap." And everybody looked at it, and built cars with 6cm gaps … and I looked at it and I thought, if that 6cm gap could be a 1cm gap I could double the downforce on the car; and it's going to go down to a 1cm gap at some point, like [under braking] at the end of the straight. So if I can make a physical thing ... that drives the car down on its own, and holds the car down on its own without any mechanical aid or button or electrics or anything, it's legal. So in three months we developed a hydro-pneumatic suspension.'

Gordon Murray's thinking on this, and he says it came as a sudden illumination, was that the authorities had to accept that at some points during a race, any car's ground clearance is going to be less than the 6cm minimum simply because of the effects of braking, or roll on corners, etc. Knowing that any driver-operated, mechanical device to alter the ground clearance was illegal, he focused on the physical forces, the basic physics, the 'bits of nature', that act on a car in motion. The braking and cornering forces he felt unable to work with because of their asymmetrical effects on the car, but the downforce from air pressure on a moving car could, if the car was correctly designed aerodynamically, push the car down equally over its whole length and width. The design challenge, therefore, was to let the natural downforce push the car down at speed, and then somehow to keep it down when it slowed for corners, and then allow the car to return to 6cm clearance at standstill.

The ingenious solution that Gordon Murray developed incorporated hydro-pneumatic suspension struts at each wheel, connected to hydraulic fluid reservoirs. As the car went faster, the natural downforce of airflow pushed the body lower on its suspension and the hydraulic fluid in each suspension strut was pushed out into the reservoirs. The trick then was to find a way of letting the fluid return to the suspension struts only very slowly when the car slowed down. At corners, the suspension would stay low, but on slowing down and stopping at the end of the race, the fluid would return from the reservoirs to the suspension struts, giving 6cm ground clearance.

'So I rushed around and looked at the technology of micro-filters, mainly in the medical industry ... they were using these organic micro-filters which let the fluid through themselves but very, very, very, slowly. And we built the world's tiniest throttle valve with one of these filters in it, and a tiny little pin – we were using drills that you couldn't even see! We went and quickly developed what size hole we needed, so that it took a lap to push the fluid through these little holes – all naturally with the downforce – pushed the fluid into the reservoirs and the car was stuck on the ground, running with its skirts virtually touching the ground. And because it took so long for the fluid to get back through the same valves and filters, it held the car down there, and after the race you have the slowing down lap … and the car just slowly came back up. Nothing to do with the driver at all, just physical forces! And we went to the first race in Argentina and just blew everybody into the weeds, just totally; and everybody went bananas!'

Other teams protested that the Brabham cars must have been fitted with a driver-operated device. It was obvious that the cars were lower during racing than they were in the pits, but of course the scrutineers could find no illegal device. Under pressure from the other teams, the authorities pointed out that the Brabham cars were clearly lower than 6cm when out on the circuit, which contravened the regulations, but Gordon countered that, at various points so was every other car. To stop the protests, he suggested to the authorities that every car should have its underbody painted, and at the end of the race every car which showed that at some point the underbody had rubbed the ground should be disqualified; and of course the other teams would not accept this.

To confuse the competition even further, Gordon Murray left the small hydraulic valve units in full view, but put a large dummy aluminium box with wires leading into the gearbox on one of the underwings of the car. 'All the teams without exception came along and tried to get the mechanics drunk and things, to try to find out what was in the box – nobody noticed the valves, and there was nothing in the box!' For some time the other teams experimented haphazardly with varieties of hydro-pneumatic suspension systems, to Gordon's amusement, but, very frustratingly for him, just a few races later in the season, FISA reversed its stance and allowed driver-operated switches for controlling suspension height.

The hydro-pneumatic suspension system was an example of an innovation initiated by a change in regulations which forced Gordon Murray's thinking onto how to retain the ground-effect advantage. It is an example of radical design innovation, through thinking from 'first principles' about the effects of natural forces, and having the motivation to follow through a basic idea into finely-detailed implementation.

## Pit Stops

Another example of radical innovation by Gordon Murray was the Brabham team's introduction of planned pit stops for refuelling during a race, before this became normal practice and was eventually ruled out in the regulations for the 2010 season. This was not so much an innovation in the car design per se, but reflects more of a systems approach to the overall goal of winning each race. At that time it was not normal to have pit stops as regular, planned parts of the race routine. Pit stops were for emergencies such as changing a punctured or badly worn tyre. For Gordon Murray, the innovation of introducing planned pit stops was part of an overall strategy arising from taking his thinking back to a basic issue – how to make the car lighter. The lighter the car, the faster it is in accelerating and decelerating.

Gordon says his mind was 'banging away' at this issue for a long time. He went to the regulations and realised that there was nothing in them about when you could put fuel into the car. So the idea dawned of running the car with only a little over half the normal, full-race fuel load, and including a pit stop for refuelling. But that was only the starting-point for a thorough investigation of the implications of such an idea, and of a working-through of the detailed implementation.

The first thing to do was to evaluate the implications of the idea. A pit stop takes a lot of time; not only is there the actual stopped time of the car at the pits, there is the time lost in decelerating and driving into the pits and also in accelerating away again on tyres that take a couple of laps to heat up to optimum operating temperature. Formula One pit stops eventually became refined down to an incredibly quick norm of about six seconds actual stopped time, in which time all four wheels were changed and maybe 100 litres of fuel taken on. The total racing time lost was perhaps some twenty seconds. Gordon calculated that if the total racing time lost by a pit stop was less than twenty-six seconds, there could be sufficient advantage gained elsewhere to make it worthwhile.

There were many factors that came into calculating the advantage. As well as the weight reduction, half-size fuel tanks also have an advantage over full-size ones in that the weight distribution is lower, and is more constant throughout the race, and the roll-couple on corners is lower, allowing faster cornering. Tyre wear, and the complicated choices of harder or softer tyre compound, also becomes a critical factor, because a lighter car can run on softer compounds which also improve cornering speeds. Even the psychology of racing came into it, because a car with obvious advantages in the early part of a race could lead other competing drivers into pushing their cars harder, or into taking more risks. For all of the objective, measurable factors, fine calculations were made, leading to the conclusion that a pit stop had to lose less than twenty-six seconds racing time to be worthwhile.

At that time, a quick pit stop for tyre changes took about fifteen seconds of actual stopped time. Gordon Murray calculated that he had to get this down to about ten seconds and to reduce as much as possible the slowing-down and warming-up times. And so, 'the innovation process continues, because you've got all these new things that nobody's done before that you have to come up with'. An extraordinary development programme had to be undertaken in an incredibly short time.

'From having the first idea to having a pit-stop car running and doing a test was three or four weeks, and that's all the time that you have. So you would take each individual thing and tackle it. Say, OK, how can we get thirty-five gallons into the car in ten seconds? The only way you're ever going to do it is using pressure, and then you have a crash programme to develop a system … That's what is great about race car design, because even though you've had the big idea – the "light bulb" thing, which is fun – the real fun is actually taking these individual things, that nobody's ever done before, and in no time at all try and think of a way of designing them. And not only think of a way of doing them, but drawing the bits, having them made and testing them.'

Within three weeks, they had thought of, designed, made and tested a pressure-fed refuelling system. To improve pit-stop procedures, Gordon hired a film crew to film the team practising pit stops, and then played back the film, stopping it to identify difficulties and errors, and devising ways to improve the procedures. Such improvements included details such as re-designing the wheel-nut gun to improve its engagement with the nut. The new systems, the improvements, and the training of the pit team got the actual stopped-time down to under the target of ten seconds. One 'big killer' remained: 'When you put new tyres on they were cold, and it always took two laps to get back up to speed, and the time you lost in those two laps killed the whole thing. So then I thought, well I know the tyres start working at seventy degrees centigrade … so we designed an oven, a wooden oven with a gas-fired heater, and we heated the tyres up, and ten seconds before the car was coming in we opened the oven door, whipped the tyres out, put them on, and the guy was instantly quick. Now every Grand Prix team has tyre heating; that's where it started.'

The example of the introduction of the 'pit-stop car' illustrates how a radical innovation was driven by the competitive urge to find a significant advantage within the constraints of the regulations; how the basic creative idea had to be evaluated on precise calculations; how a total systems approach was adopted; and how implementation had to be carried through to fine levels of detail.

## F1 Steering Column

The McLaren F1 sports car was designed on Formula One principles, and included many radical innovations. One of these was the interior seating layout, with the driver seated centrally and two passenger seats positioned slightly rearward and overlapping with the driver's seat. This 'arrowhead' layout was something that Gordon had had in mind for many years, as evidenced by a sketch in his student notebook, some twenty-five years earlier! It is a very visible example of how he is prepared always to think anew about any aspect of the car that he is designing.

As a less-visible example of his approach to designing from first principles, Gordon refers to a small and perhaps seemingly insignificant part of the McLaren F1, the steering column. 'Conventionally, it would have been, right, steering columns are typically three-quarter-inch solid steel bars.' He explained how this conventional solution arises because the column not only has to carry torsional forces from the resistance to the turning wheels but also bending loads from the driver leaning on it while getting in and out of the car. It also has conventional points of support, is mounted in rubber bushes to reduce noise, and it ends up being encased in a plastic housing for reasons of appearance and convenience. But it does not provide the sort of direct steering feel that a racing driver needs, and the McLaren F1 is supposed to be a driver's car.

So Gordon decided to apply racing design principles, starting by separating the needs to carry both torque and bending loads. Whatever the form of the steering column itself, it still needs a cover to house electrical cables and to mount switches, 'so if you've got to have that anyway, why not use the insect principle where the skeleton's on the outside, and make that the structure that takes all the bending forces?' This thinking led to the design of the steering column itself as an aluminium tube of just 1mm wall thickness; 'it's only taking torque and it weighs nothing'. The steering rack is cast integrally with the bulkhead, so that there can be no relative movement. The support bush is right behind the steering wheel rather than down at the dashboard, and the system is now lighter but stronger than a conventional solution, and also has the right racing feel (Figure 2.3). The design process stemmed from considering first principles – separating the torque and bending loads – and from an imaginative breakthrough – using the housing cover for structural purposes as well as appearance and practicality.

Gordon Murray insists on keeping experience 'at the back of your mind, not the front' and to work from first principles when designing. For instance, in designing a component such as a suspension wishbone, he says, 'It's all too easy, and the longer you're in design the easier it is to say, I know all about wishbones, this is how it's going to look because that's what wishbones look like.' But if you want to make a step forward, if you're looking for ways of making it much better and much lighter, then you have to go right back to engineering analysis. He says it is like always designing things as though for the first time, rather than the $n$-th time.

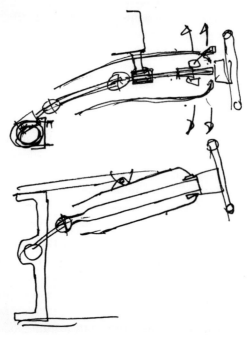

**2.3** Gordon Murray's explanatory sketch of the F1 steering column design. Top: the F1, with an 'exo-skeleton' structural external casing to house cables and hold switches, and a rigidly-mounted small, light steering column; Bottom: a conventional design, with a heavy, solid column inside a light casing.

## City Car Design

Gordon Murray is known principally as a racing car designer. But for many years he nursed a very different concept of what a car could be – a small, cheap, city-car. After he left McLaren he began development of this very different kind of car in his own design company. The resulting concept was finally announced in 2008 as the T.25 city car, and the first prototype was built in 2010. The T.25 is a very practical urban-use vehicle that can carry a driver with two passengers or a large amount of luggage or shopping; it is light and agile, with good performance and low fuel consumption, and occupies one-third of the road or parking space of a conventional car. However, Gordon Murray's motivation for designing the T.25 was not so much the economic and environmental advantages it might offer, but a desire to design an efficient, small car that would be attractive and fun to drive, and would radically impact traffic problems such as congestion. His aim was to develop not just a new type of car but a new concept of personal transport.

Just as in his racing car design work, the city car is also designed from first principles. This is clear in some of Gordon's earliest sketches for the car (Figure 2.4), dating from the early 1990s, in which he pays special attention to the suspension system. The suspension system is an important feature in early considerations because a tall, narrow car such as the T.25 tends to roll sideways on corners, and that has to be countered in the suspension system.

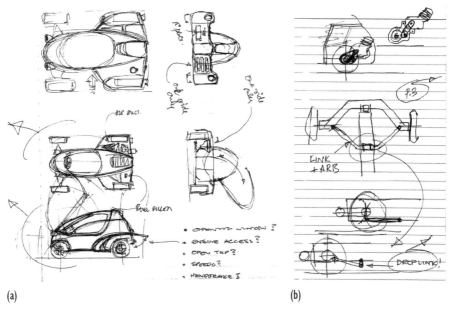

(a)                                            (b)

**2.4** Some of Gordon Murray's early sketches for the city car concept: (a) overall concept, (b) a very early sketch of suspension and other details, made in a pocket notebook, around the same time as the concept sketches.

He also explained that, for economy, 'I want to make a suspension with the least number of components and moving parts; this has only three parts in the whole suspension system.' The same kind of thinking applied also, for example, to the initial 'frog eye' headlight design. 'It's not just styling, it's a practical point of view, because I only want to have one sub-wiring loop for cost, so I want to put the [rear-view] mirror in the back of the light, so you have headlamp, parking lamp, main beam, low beam, indicators, side repeater, heating element, adjusting element for the mirror, and the mirror, on one sub-loop with one plastic plug, so you have one moulded pod that does all those things, all those functions.'

In fact, for this city car the innovative manufacturing concept is as important as the innovative design concept. This integrated thinking is essential to his approach to designing a low-cost solution, as he explains: 'You need something that is small, light, radical, efficient, and it has to be cheap, because one thing you can't do is build the world's most sophisticated little city car that will save the world and then say to people it costs £17,000, because you won't sell many – if you don't sell enough it won't make a difference, and the way you reduce the cost of producing a car and therefore the retail price is by first of all reducing the part count, the number of parts that go into the car, and that you do by design and by conceptual design.' So for Gordon Murray conceptual design, detail design and manufacturing are all tightly bound together.

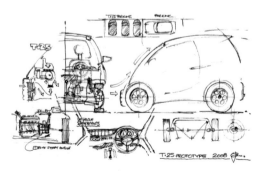

**2.5** Later sketches for the T.25 city car.

Even a radical concept such as the easy-access, single, lift-up opening canopy, rather than side doors, came from the same approach. 'Going from seven openings to five makes a car a lot cheaper and more rigid and lighter; going from five to three and from three to two is magic, and going down to one you can't get any better – you've got to get into the car. So that sort of stuff you think about from the beginning, and that applies to lights, mirrors, instruments, wheels, brakes, everything.'

After producing many dozens of small sketches of details and concepts over several years (Figure 2.5), and experimenting with performance, using different engines in some existing small cars, the design work took a major step forward when Gordon and his team built a very simple, full-size mock-up of the car, using wire and cardboard (Figure 2.6). The final version of the city car (Figure 2.7) bore a striking resemblance to that simple mock-up. The mock-up became a useful design tool, as it began to suggest some new possibilities. For example, Gordon's earlier idea for the seating arrangement was for two people sitting in tandem, the passenger behind the driver. But when the mock-up was built, 'we discovered that you could, quite easily with the same width of motor car, for short journeys, you could take three people in it', using a similar seating layout as in the McLaren F1. Another cost-saving idea also arose from exploring the mock-up, when one of the team realised that the rear-located engine could be accessed from inside the car, so avoiding the need for an external access. Gordon explained that, 'At one stage, we were looking at having to have a boot lid to access the engine, until one of the guys said, Come and look at this, if you stand in the car you can open what is effectively your boot floor from the inside of the car, you can get to the oil and water and stuff from there – if you fold the seats flat, open the hatch in the floor and you are there.'

In the city car design we can see that the same kind of design thinking is applied by Gordon Murray as in his racing car design. There is a fine attention to detail, that interlocks with the overall concept and can trigger some of the big ideas as well as the little ones. And there is a breadth of approach towards an overall goal that is greater than the apparent focus of attention, the car itself.

**2.6** The early wire and card mock-up for the city car, showing the single opening canopy.

**2.7** The first prototype version of the T.25 city car.

## Learning from Failures

For Gordon Murray, it is the pressure of competitive design and the necessity to follow-through ideas into rigid implementation that results in successful innovation. He suspects that many people have 'bright ideas', but that they lack the experience and the motivation to carry it through to fruition: 'They have this great idea and then they lose interest.'

However, he also admits that not all his racing car design innovations have been successes; he has had a share of failures, too. One of his largest failures was the Brabham 'surface cooling' car. This radical concept was meant to be several steps forward at once; reduction in weight, improvement in driver safety, and what was meant to be a long-term technical advantage over the opposition. His imaginative idea of 'surface cooling' was to do away with normal radiators for cooling the engine, and instead to pass the water and oil through surface heat exchangers built integrally into the monocoque structure: the 'skin' of the car was both structure and radiator. Other refinements included improved monocoque form, elaborate electronic engine and lap-time instrumentation systems for the driver, carbon-fibre brake discs, and an on-board air jacking system for quicker tyre changes.

There were innumerable detailed implementation problems with the surface cooling features, and trials soon showed that surface cooling was not going to work. Gordon said, 'I knew why it didn't work, but before the first race we just literally ran out of time.' So a revamped version of the previous season's car was quickly rushed out. It had been a very expensive failure.

Another innovative design that failed was the last one Gordon Murray designed for Brabham, for the 1986 season. This car was designed to be as low as possible, with the driver almost lying flat. It involved also putting the engine into a reclined position, and this was the feature that proved not to work. 'We just could not get the lay-down engine to scavenge the oil properly, and we kept losing a lot of horsepower.' Later, at McLaren for the 1988 season he was able to develop the same concept more successfully; 'I did a lay-down McLaren, exactly what we did at Brabham but with a Honda engine that worked, and we won fifteen out of sixteen races. So you do have things that don't work; but in that case it wasn't the idea that didn't work, I just ran out of time and money, and I took on much too much in a very short period to get it to work properly.'

## Design Process and Working Methods

Although Gordon Murray carried immense personal responsibility for the design work of his racing cars, and of course for his city car, for which he founded his own company, inevitably it involved a lot of teamwork. Clearly he has been successful in inspiring others to work with him. He likes to involve team members in the design problems, and for that reason prefers to recruit all-rounders to his team: 'I never have engineers that aren't designers.' He also likes to work collectively, standing around a drawing board or a mock-up discussing problems and trying ideas. For the McLaren F1 design, he installed a five-metre-long drawing board in the design office, so that the car could be drawn full size, and several team members at once could gather round and contribute.

As for managing a team, he regards it as treading a fine line between dictator and diplomat. He knows exactly what he wants to achieve, but he likes being able to have people around 'to bounce ideas off'. He prefers being able to hand-pick a team, and to give his people enough freedom and responsibility to feel that they are really making a worthwhile contribution to the team. His personal motivation manifests itself in a dedication which he also expects to find in the other members of his design team; he expects to appoint people who, 'if you cut them, they bleed motor oil'. Because everyone is dedicated to the team cause, he finds no need, for example, to run a separate research and development section; everyone is motivated enough to keep up to date constantly with new developments and new technology, and feeding information and ideas into the team.

Gordon's personal design process is based on starting with a quick sketch of a whole idea, which is then developed through many different refinements. He said that, 'I do a quick sketch of the whole idea, and then if there's one bit that looks good, instead of rubbing other bits out, I'd put that bit to one side; I'd do it again and expand on the good bit, and drop out the bad bit, and keep doing it, doing it; and end up with all these sketches, and eventually you end up throwing ninety percent of these away.' He also talks to himself – or rather, writes notes to himself on the sketches; notes such as 'rubbish', 'too heavy' or 'move it this way 30mm'. Eventually he gets to the stage of more formal, orthographic drawings, but still drawing annotated plans, elevations and sections all together, 'Until at the end of the day the guys at Brabham used to call them "Gordon's Wonder Plots", because they used to say "It's a wonder anybody could see what was in them"!'

# 3

# Designing to Please

This second case study is based on interviews with another outstanding designer, the product designer Kenneth Grange. As with the previous chapter, the main purpose in making this study is to seek insight into the design thinking of someone who is a successful, innovative designer.

Kenneth Grange was a founding partner in the world-renowned interdisciplinary design consultancy Pentagram. He is a well-known and highly successful designer of a great variety of products that range in scale from ballpoint pens and disposable razors to taxi cabs and railway engines. His career has spanned more than fifty years, and many of his designs became (and remain) familiar items in the household or on the street – or on the rail track. These designs include food mixers for Kenwood, razors for Wilkinson Sword, cameras for Kodak, typewriters for Imperial, clothes irons for Morphy Richards, cigarette lighters for Ronson, washing machines for Bendix, pens for Parker, lamps for Anglepoise, the front end of the British Rail high-speed train, and the innovative TX1 version of the famous London taxi-cab. He is one of the Royal Society of Arts' élite corps of 'Royal Designers for Industry', and his designs have won ten Design Council Awards and the Duke of Edinburgh's prize for elegant Design. He has won the Gold Medal of the Chartered Society of Designers, and in 2001 he was awarded the Prince Philip Designers Prize – an award honouring lifetime achievement.

## Background

A curious thing about Kenneth Grange's highly successful career is that it appears to have started and developed initially by a series of accidents. The son of a policeman, the fourteen-year-old Kenneth 'volunteered' at school to apply for a scholarship to Art School. After four years at Willesden School of Arts and Crafts, where 'all I really learned was draughtsmanship', and a short job as a scene painter with BBC television, he was recommended by the principal of the art school to 'go and see a woman who had been a student with him and who was working in the Institute of Town Planning'. This contact in turn recommended him to some architect friends of hers, who turned out to be the firm of Arcon, a leading progressive architectural firm of that era. Kenneth recalls that 'I had never heard of architecture, I hadn't the slightest idea of what this meant, but they gave me a job in what they called their technical publications department', making presentation drawings for clients.

Kenneth was then soon after, at age nineteen, subject to two years of conscription into the British Army, where his 'little portfolio' of drawings got him allocated, not to painting camouflage on tanks as he might have expected, but as an illustrator producing drawings for instruction manuals. This work involved taking apart, usually by personal trial and error, various artillery mechanisms, and then making drawings to illustrate the parts and their assembly. 'You had to draw them in such a way, assemble the drawings in such a way, that it was a re-assembly process that you were explaining.' This self-instruction in the assembly and re-assembly of military machines became

Kenneth's introduction to engineering, and the beginning of his fascination with the way things work, with the necessities of practicality and function that became underlying principles of his approach to design. He says, 'I think you have it in your genes to be inquisitive – practical I suppose is the word you might use, but there's a fundamental interest in mechanics and structures and things that you have or you don't have.'

After leaving the Army, Kenneth returned to his architect colleagues for work. One of the Arcon partners, Jack Howe, encouraged Kenneth to undertake some independent work of his own. These private jobs were mostly 'week-ends painting a mural or whatever. But somehow I picked up a little tiny job which was doing an exhibition for the then Atomic Energy Authority.' This little job was so successful that the client called him again some months later, to say 'We've taken space at an exhibition in Geneva, and would you like to design the exhibition stand for us?' The new job turned out to be too large for Kenneth to be able to cope with on his own, 'but within a month I'd got three people working for me full-time, and we were working in my flat, we'd taken over the living-room as well as the little office-workshop I'd got, and with every week the job increased. It turned into a big, big job.' And so the Kenneth Grange design consultancy was accidentally up and running.

## Product Innovations

A significant feature of much of Kenneth Grange's design work is that it is not based on just the styling or re-styling of a product. His designs often arise from a fundamental reassessment of the purpose, function and use of the product. However, this radical, innovative ability is not necessarily the reason why clients invite him to take on a new job. He says, 'You are invariably brought in by somebody who has got a very elementary commercial motive in changing the perception of the product. It's extremely unusual for someone to be brought in to approach it from this usability, this function theme.' But he feels the need for a 'secure foundation' when starting a new project, and that foundation is the product functionality. 'I am never daunted by the blank sheet of paper because I know I can at least fill in my time by trying to sort out just the functionality, just the handling of it, and by-and-large out of that comes a direction, and then it's a question of tuning. I think it's back to what your temperament is, your personality. I think with my background and my own knowledge about my weaknesses I am bound to need to have a secure foundation on which I stand when I am arguing about something, and I am not very comfortable when I find myself required to be the prima donna.'

His practical attitude towards product functionality also extends into his normal, everyday life. 'As I get older I get less and less tolerant of things that don't work easily, and so I think I go around looking for trouble!' As an example, he recounts a recent experience in a restaurant, specialising in serving mussels: 'The waiter comes along and dumps on the table a big stainless steel bowl [of mussels] with a lid, and this is hot. My companion's lid had handles on it, and mine didn't have handles on it. That made me furious, and I alone in that restaurant – probably they have never had anybody else complain about it – but not Grange – he shouts and hollers and tells the waiter and calls for the manager. I can't resist it, because I find that so much like a real affront!'

## Frister & Rossman Sewing Machine

Being affronted by the poor usability of a product means that in his own design work Kenneth inevitably puts usability at the forefront of his thinking. A clear example of this is provided by his design of a sewing machine for Frister & Rossman, a firm based in Germany producing high-quality, well-engineered machines but who were looking for new designs to stimulate sales. Kenneth's resulting design incorporated the standard machinery, but repackaged it in novel ways that made the machine easier to use and gave it a new and distinctive form and style (Figure 3.1).

The origins of the new design features lay in Kenneth's functional, practical approach, and on his personal experience. His starting point was his own use of a sewing machine: 'I chose to use it, actually making things with a sewing machine, so I did fairly quickly come to understand just fundamental

**3.1** The Frister & Rossman sewing machine designed by Kenneth Grange.

strengths and weaknesses.' He found what he regarded as a 'contradiction' in the conventional design. The sewing machine mechanism is conventionally located centrally on its base platform, whereas the user needs more surface space on their side of the needle than behind it. He explained that, 'In front of the needle, the longer the table on which you can actually assemble and lay and just get the tension of the fabrics right, the better. Once the work is behind the needle you can do nothing about it, it's sewn, therefore you don't need any space for the fabric.' Kenneth therefore simply moved the sewing machine mechanism rearwards on its base, creating an off-centre layout with more base-table space in front of the needle than behind it. To him, this appeared a virtually self-evident improvement to make: 'This is such a straightforward thing to do, but the reason it had not been done before was because the sewing machine had been designed as a very straightforward, basic piece of engineering which needed stability. Therefore the mechanism was from the very beginning put centrally upon the base and nobody had thought about challenging the space beyond and the space in front of the needle.' Once this challenge had been met, and the benefit of an off-centre layout perceived, then 'the rest of the shape follows, the rest of the shape just absolutely falls into place from that'.

Another radical change in this particular sewing machine design was also a result of a simple, fundamental assessment of how the machine is used. Kenneth gave the base of the machine radiused lower edges, which might look like a mere 'styling' feature, but in fact also arose from function. 'There was something that they told me, which is that a frequent problem with sewing machines, particularly when you are sewing a new fabric, is that a lot of lint comes off the fabric, loose fibres and so on. This gets down into the bobbin and at worst stops the machine, at best will get itself sewn back into the thing, so you haven't got an absolutely clean stitch, which affects the tension, the thread, etc. And they said, this is a problem, and their way of dealing with it was to make sure you could open the front and get the bobbin out.' This was achieved by the user tilting the machine backwards, away from them, into a rather unstable position that only allowed restricted access to the shuttle mechanism in the underside of the base.

To Kenneth Grange, this was simply inadequate. 'I thought, that doesn't seem to me to be very clever, why don't we make sure we can open the thing and really get at it? So I tilted the thing sideways, I rolled the whole thing back so it stood up and was very firm, and you could get the whole of the guts apart and get at the lint and so on, and that in itself generated a shape because then the back edge of the machine naturally had a roll to it.' The rolled edge made it easier for the user to tilt the machine, it rested more stable and secure, and the underside was accessible for cleaning and oiling the lower mechanisms. A radiused top front edge was also provided to the base plate, to allow the fabric to slide over it more easily, and various other features were added, such as small drawers for holding accessories. Kenneth's sketches, illustrating his approach, are shown in Figure 3.2.

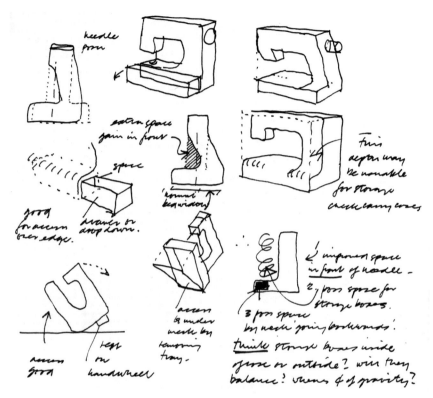

**3.2** Kenneth Grange's sketches summarising some of the principles underlying his design of the sewing machine.

The sewing machine design demonstrates how Kenneth Grange approaches design from a functional viewpoint. The innovative 'style' and features of the new machine were generated from considering and responding to the normal patterns of its use. He says, 'I think it's a question of what your attitude is towards anything, any working thing. My attitude is to want it to be a pleasure to operate.' Another aspect of this approach is that he considers the whole pattern of use, as exemplified by considering the requirements of periodically cleaning the machine, and by considering how the user prepares and introduces the fabric into the stitching mechanism, thus requiring more make-up space in front of the needle than behind it. It is a fundamental part of his interest in how things work: 'Those are the things that intrigue me, recognising that there is a difference between what happens after a particular process and what happens before it, and so on, and preparing yourself for those two stages.'

However, it is interesting to know that Kenneth was very unsure about presenting his radical design proposals to his clients. These were actually the directors of the company that owned Frister & Rossman, the Maruzen company, based in Osaka, Japan. After being briefed by them in Osaka, he returned to England to start the design work, and actually developed two different designs. One was the radical design, and the other was more con-servative – 'It created a new form, but followed the brief precisely and did not alter the basic layout of the mechanics.' Kenneth returned to Osaka with models of both designs. 'The night before I was due to present my proposal, I looked long and hard at the two versions. I was afraid of looking foolish should some blindingly obvious reason be revealed for not deviating from the original brief. Only when I left my room the following morning did I decide to opt for excitement and take them the non-briefed model. In the event, they were very impressed.'

## British Rail High Speed Train

Going well beyond the requirements of the original brief was also a major feature of one of Kenneth Grange's most prestigious and long-lasting designs, the front bodywork of the High Speed Train introduced into passenger service by British Rail in 1975. It was perhaps surprising for a product designer, usu-ally working on much smaller machines and devices, to find himself involved in the design of such a major engineering product, but again the example illustrates Kenneth's functional approach and eagerness to do what seems necessary, rather than just what is asked for.

The High Speed Train (HST) was developed within British Rail as a kind of internal rival to the much-vaunted, radical Advanced Passenger Train (APT) being developed at the same period, which used revolutionary new technologies such as tilting carriages to increase running speeds. The APT eventually failed altogether, whereas the HST, using evolutionary develop-ments of conventional engineering (and some APT innovations), became hugely successful and, in its 1973 prototype version, with the Grange-designed nose cone, set a world speed record for diesel traction of 230 km/h.

Kenneth recalls that 'They didn't call me up and say, We'd like you to design a locomotive.' It began much more modestly, as a result of some smaller jobs that he had undertaken for the railways, such as re-designing the timetables. 'I had done a number of jobs for the railways, all quite modest jobs, but one or two of them quite important; like I was responsible for changing the basic format of timetabling. When I was asked to redesign a timetable for them, it was one of those printed sheets that you got, organised from purely the point of view of the driver, which is the way the railways grew up. They were actually drivers' schedules; they didn't start by telling you where the train was going, they started by telling you what time the trains went out, and which track, the departure track. Further down was where the thing was going, if you took the time to read it all; it was a list of where the stops were, which is not the way to organise a timetable. The person rushing into the station, the only thing he knows is where he is going, you want to be able to look up your destination and then see the time of the train, but it was exactly the other way around.' So Kenneth re-designed the timetable so that 'Where you are going comes first, and after that comes the time the train leaves.'

After a few such 'little' jobs, Kenneth was approached by his British Rail client representative, James Cousins, Head of the Design Department, about 'a paint job, the painting of the outside of a train'. This train was the new HST. 'So I went in to see him and he had a model there, and it was a model of a very crude bullet-nosed train, and he said to me, This is being produced by the Engineering Department at Derby, this is the train they intend to make, but I can't possibly let them get away with this awful paintwork. It had zig-zags on, and so he said, Please come back with a proposal for the painting of this train. I went away and I did that but I also thought, I could improve the shape of this.' The brief, therefore, was for a styling contribution – a paint livery that might improve the appearance of the train. But Kenneth was not satisfied with such a restricted 'styling contribution': he wanted the style to emerge from the function, and so, without telling Cousins, he found an aerodynamicist, and managed to get use of a wind tunnel test facility at Imperial College, London, and began to make a series of models of the front of the train, gradually developing a better, more efficient, overall shape.

'So bit by bit we developed an evolution of the shape of the train, based upon wind tunnel testing. I then went along to Cousins with this information and I said, Here's some photos of a shape that's not your bullet-nose, but it's a shape that I think is much more elegant, and by the way, here's the paint job. And he went into a meeting with the Board, and when this thing came up on the agenda he said, Here's the model and here's the livery I propose, but we have taken the liberty of doing some preliminary work on the shape; we believe that the shape proposed – nothing to do with the [engineering of the] running gear, with the actual motor, and so on – but we believe the shape actually could be more efficient. And he had wind tunnel photographs and the Engineering Department had never been near a wind tunnel! I wish I had been in the meeting, I'm sure it was a real landmark meeting, when the Board was persuaded by these photos in the wind tunnel. Then afterwards he came out of the meeting and came back and said, Well, we have a job to do! But the rest was then relatively easy.'

A successful prototype was developed to Kenneth's design, but the story did not end there. 'I had kept strictly within the technical terms of the brief. This dictated a window made of exceptionally strong flat glass, which severely limited its size, and a single driver's seat positioned centrally. But instead of production going ahead with my design, a disagreement arose between the union and management which resulted in a decision to position a driver and co-driver side by side. This had a profound effect on the design, since our aerodynamics, vindicated by the speed record, relied on a smooth flow of air to left and right of the front window.' There was a number of interrelated problems raised by the necessity of providing for two side-by-side operators at the front of the cab, instead of the one central operator. The central, relatively small window in the prototype would have to be replaced by two windows with a central bar, and the extra window width inevitably flattened the front profile, thus reducing the aerodynamic efficiency. Even when the glassmakers found that a larger, single sheet of the toughened glass could be produced, the aerodynamic problem was still there.

One way of regaining the aerodynamic efficiency appeared to be to elongate and lower the rake of the cab-front, so as to direct more air up and over the top rather than around the sides. But this option was denied by the technical requirement of providing the engine's buffers at the front, which were located in a fixed position relative to the wheel bogies, and could not be fully enclosed. Train buffers are necessary not, as is often thought, to cushion the train's stop at the end of the track, but to assist the engine to shunt carriages around in the assembling of complete trains.

Kenneth was unhappy about losing the aerodynamic efficiency, and pursued the matter with the railways' Chief Engineer. 'Credit is due to the Chief Engineer, because I wasn't welcomed by these guys, but to this man's everlasting credit I was sitting in a meeting with him, going over this fact that this new design was not as efficient as the one that they originally bought, and which had already set a world record. But there is no way you can have the geometry and have the wide window and get the same effect, and we were backwards and forwards over this. I suppose I knew that if we didn't have buffers I'd get a different shape, so I said to him, Tell me again, tell me about buffers, how they work; thinking there might be some way I could sleek them in somehow or other. But you see, you've got this great plate and you've got probably fifteen inches of movement on the springs because of the shunting, and all that's got to be on its own stalk, you can't have that inside a housing, really it's got to be outside of the housing. And he said, Well, it is true that with this vehicle, which we've never, ever made before, we've never, ever made a train where the coaches are always attached, with this, of course, they'll always stay coupled. And he said, So if it's always coupled, it can't be used for shunting, and therefore the only thing we need is a hard link. And so he said, So really we don't need the buffers. To his credit he was prepared to say, We've overlooked it. They'd never, ever made a complete train like that before – they made locomotives, and they made carriages.' The evolution of the HST design is illustrated in Figure 3.3.

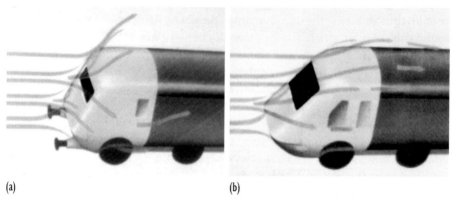

(a)                                              (b)

**3.3** Development of the nose of the High Speed Train to improve aerodynamics: (a) rounded nose with buffers; (b) raked nose without buffers.

Kenneth's perseverance had led to the vital breakthrough. The buffers on this locomotive for a new, permanently-coupled train, could be dispensed with. The aerodynamic efficiency could be retained by diverting the airflow from around the sides to over the top of a sleeker, more stylish, cab front. British Rail had a completely new, modern image, arising from its original request for 'a paint job'.

## Learning from Failures

Like Gordon Murray, Kenneth Grange is also ready to admit that he has produced some designs that failed, and to hope that he has learned from such failures. One example comes from his design for the Channel Tunnel Eurostar train, running between Britain and continental Europe. Kenneth was one of four designers invited to submit proposals, and he felt confident of winning the competition, given his previous experience with the High Speed Train. He worked on two designs, one with a 'bubble' windscreen for the driver, and one much closer to the HST shape. He says that, 'Because I thought the train was a sort of natural son of the HST, I abandoned the bubble idea.' But he lost the competition to someone who produced a design based around a 'bubble' windscreen! Kenneth suggests that 'The real blunder for me was to have even thought of a reference to the HST. Clearly the French and the Belgian partners must certainly not have wanted a son of the British national train on "their" railways!'

Another railway-related design failure for Kenneth was the 'net chair' he designed for British Rail. The goal was to produce a very lightweight seat that would make a significant contribution to reducing the overall weight of a railway carriage. Kenneth found a net fabric used in spacecraft design, and produced a highly ergonomic, comfortable and very lightweight seat in which the net fabric was the primary support for the user. But unfortunately the seat was highly vulnerable to vandalism. 'We had reckoned without the spite of the travelling yobbo who, with one quick slash of a knife, destroyed the seat.'

## Design Process and Working Methods

The examples of the Frister & Rossman sewing machine and the British Rail High Speed Train illustrate Kenneth Grange's approach to design, which seems predominantly to be based on generating style and form from function and use. This seems to be the natural way for him to work, even though his clients sometimes do not realise this, and approach him as a 'stylist'. 'They think,' he says, 'We need a new design, we need a new style. They're sharp enough to realise the style is outdated or whatever, and they assume because of what they have seen that it's a purely artistic thing, it's a fashion thing only to do with style. I can't get to a solution from that beginning, so I start entirely from the point of view of, can I make the use of the thing better. Eventually, by some extraordinary piece of good fortune, I wind up with a style that they think is terrific and how it got there they are not interested. It does become interesting when we then start to develop it because I find I'm defending bits of the mechanistic process and they don't want me to, particularly the engineers don't want me to!' He says he always has a concern with 'the nitty-gritty' of products and their use, including not only their primary function but also secondary aspects such as their cleaning. And yet he rejects what he sometimes sees in others as 'a highly moral stance where function is all.' There has been a temptation, he says, for some designers 'to scorn the elements of style, fashion and pleasure. That, in my view, is the road to righteous boredom.'

In addition to this personal commitment, however, he frequently refers to the 'happy accidents' that seem to have dominated his career. 'I keep saying accident, but it is – I happen to be on the scene when people need a particular skill, and I am of the good fortune to be on the doorstep, passing the front door when that particular skill is needed. An example of this casualness, as I call it, is in both the train and in the design I did for the Chef [the Kenwood Chef food mixer – one of Kenneth's earliest and most well-known designs], which eventually led me to 35 years of working with Kenwood. I got the job of designing the Chef because I said I'd do it in three days, and my money was probably the least of the three people they were talking to. And the casualness, by which the thing was accepted, and then goes into production, and my whole life opens up, is that with only three days in which to do it, I had three days and two nights, and the only method I knew, because I'd never had any training as a designer, although a good draughtsman I'd never had any of the skilful training about presentation drawing, so I wasn't good at flashy drawings and things and I did everything with model-making, every single thing I did with model-making because I could do it, personally do it. I didn't have enough time, I only had time enough to make half a model, just could not make a whole model, so I made a half and I took a mirror with me [to produce the effect of seeing the symmetrical whole]. Now it wasn't artifice on my part, at least it wasn't a trick, it was just a practical way of showing them a whole thing with half the effort. Kenneth Wood loved it, and I think he loved it because he thought it was salesmanship. For me, it was a pure bit of good luck.'

# 4

# How Designers Think

This chapter will summarise and compare the observations we can make and the lessons we can draw from the two case studies of outstanding designers, Gordon Murray and Kenneth Grange. Although they stem from very different domains of design – racing car, city car, sewing machine, locomotive – the examples in our two case studies can be seen to have similarities in the approaches taken by the designers. Some of these similarities seem to stem from their backgrounds and personalities, and they obviously share personal, highly motivated attitudes towards their work and the achievement of success. We can also compare their approaches with those of other successful designers, by drawing upon some of the other studies that have been made of such designers. And we can begin to generalise about what can be learned from these designer studies in terms of aspects of design thinking that they all seem to adopt.

## Motivation and Attitude

Gordon Murray thinks that innovative design, certainly in motor racing, starts with 'a certain type of person', like himself, who has a strong desire to beat the opposition: 'All you want to do is go back next time and blow them all into the weeds.' Not all racing car designers are like that, he agrees, but he has always had that strong competitive urge. The strength of his personal motivation cannot be doubted; it would have been essential to carry him through so many innovations, through failures as well as successes, in such a highly pressured environment. He has also had a strong personal interest and involvement in motor racing and car design throughout his life, including designing, building and racing his own sports car as a young man. The novel three-seat driver/passengers layout of the McLaren F1, used again in the city car, in which the driver is central and two passengers are side-by-side slightly behind the driver, is something that featured in his design sketchbooks as a teenager, and he says that other ideas are still there waiting for an opportunity to be realised.

Kenneth Grange's approach to design also seems to be rooted in his early experiences of 'learning by doing' – of learning to take apart and re-assemble artillery mechanisms so that he could make the drawings to allow someone else to do it. Another relevant aspect of his time in the Army, he believes, was that it helped develop his physical health and strength, which he regards as a key to the hard work and long hours he later put into building and running his design practice. This physical aptitude is part of the strength of leadership, he believes: 'I think a large part of the ability of any team to achieve anything is a mixture of resources – obviously intellectual resource is a very important part, but then there are resources which are simply to do with whether you can stay awake, and stay awake at a keen, high, top level of concentration. So I think inevitably there's a question of teams following the physical and behavioural examples of the leader.'

Kenneth also has strong personal motivation and what he calls an 'I can do it' attitude: 'I think there's a bit of me that is a commercial animal I suppose, a bit of me that's certainly an "I can do it" man, under any circumstances.

I always say yes, and of course it gets me into trouble!' This personal commitment also helps in the leadership of his design teams, he believes. 'I think that's what builds the team; they know back at the ranch that this man Grange is out there saying, "Yes we can do it tomorrow!" And the likelihood therefore is that they're not going to see the girlfriend tonight, and they know every day might be the same.'

As chief designer, it seems necessary to have a lot of self-confidence to carry-through new ideas in a highly pressured environment. It involves taking risk, and shouldering a lot of responsibility. Gordon Murray finds that this personal responsibility naturally brings intense psychological pressure: 'There are patches of loneliness really, when you sit there and think, I'm committing all next year's budget, there are all the mechanics relying on me, all the team, all the sponsors, all the drivers, friends, family – I mean, the car's got to go well, and I'm committed to this loony idea, you know?' Even he admits to feeling sometimes very nervous about the risks he was taking: 'Occasionally you wake up in the night and think, phew, maybe I'll do a normal car!' But for him, that risk-taking is the difference between the innovative and non-innovative designer. The speed and pressure and commitment of racing car design are such that adrenaline and an almost physical exhilaration kept him going: 'It's like surfing on top of a wave, and you know you can't get off.' It's clear that he also carried this attitude through into designing the city car, self-imposing the pressure to produce a radical new concept of personal transport.

In explaining his approach to innovative design, Gordon Murray stresses the need constantly to work from 'first principles'. In Formula One racing, he was often surprised to find that other teams were not taking such a basic approach, and that they would frequently merely copy the successful innovations of someone else. Working from first principles, and working in a highly organised way seem to come naturally to him, but his personal design process is much less structured than the results might suggest. Although he can tightly organise his team and run a complex racing organisation, his personal ways of designing are relatively unstructured, based on annotated, thumbnail sketches. 'I don't sit down and say, OK, now I've had the idea, let's see, this is a solution, these are the different ways to go, if I do this, and do that; I do lots of scribbles just to save it, before I forget.'

For Kenneth Grange, his innovative design work often stems from going beyond the original brief, and that experience helped form his sceptical attitude towards developing and following a tight initial specification. The designer's job, he says, is 'to produce the unexpected'. And that does not happen by trying to 'get the brief right, go through the process in an orderly fashion, check that you have done what you have been told to do'. Instead, 'It's the little bits of inspiration, the little sort of byways and the unlikely analogies and things that eventually produce what you recognise as being the right thing to do.' He suggests that 'No brief of itself ever produced an unexpected market leader. Success lies in finding the chinks in the specifications and reaching through to the concealed plums.'

It is as though his ability is primarily perceptual, a way of seeing; not something that he has to work and worry at until he gets an idea, and not something that emerges in the process of designing so much as the process of initial problem formulation. He agrees with this interpretation: 'You do have to ferret around, which is like an intellectual bit of it, to see, to find that which is then suddenly obvious to you, and I think that has happened very often. Sometimes you almost have to fabricate the problem.' He reinterprets, or brings a fresh perception to the design problem so as to establish a new concept, and the rest is working this through; the perceptive insight gives 'a direction, and then it's a question of tuning'.

## Other Outstanding Designers

These two case studies also reinforce and resonate with many of the observations that have been made in other studies of successful, innovative designers, and extend even further across the range of fields of design in which they practice.

In Chapter 1, I drew upon the interviews that Bryan Lawson conducted with some highly successful, creative architects. He drew attention to similarities in the working methods of the architects he studied, which also have similarities with the engineering designer Gordon Murray and the product designer Kenneth Grange. One such is the need to maintain periods of intense activity, but interspersed with periods, usually away from the normal work environment, of more reflective contemplation. Lawson's architects also are characterised by a dedicated sense of purpose, which they share with small, highly motivated teams of co-workers. There is also a common sense of focusing on a problem so precisely that it can be approached from 'first principles'; as the outstanding engineer-architect Santiago Calatrava was reported by Lawson to say: 'It is the answer to a particular problem that makes the work of the engineer ... you need a very precise problem.'

One thing that emerges strongly from Lawson's studies that resonates with the study of Gordon Murray is the architects' use of drawing as a design aid. Lawson observed that, 'Frequently, drawings are overlaid and mixed together. Two-dimensional plans or sections can be seen with sketches and more diagrammatic marks all on the same piece of paper in what appears a confusing jumble.' These sound very much like Gordon's 'Wonder Plots'. The architects also use their drawings as a means of 'thinking aloud', or 'talking to themselves', as Gordon put it. For example, as the architect Richard MacCormac said, 'I use drawing as a process of criticism and discovery', which sounds very similar to Gordon's approach. The common elements in these similar approaches are the use of drawing not only as a means of externalising cognitive images but also of actively 'thinking by drawing', and of responding, layer after layer and view after view, to the design as it emerges in the drawings.

Another study of an innovative designer, by Linda Candy and Ernest Edmonds, is particularly relevant because, like our study of Gordon Murray, it was also based upon the design of race-winning competition vehicles. Candy and Edmonds studied the design process of the racing-bicycle designer, Mike Burrows. His innovative, carbon-fibre, single-piece 'monocoque' frame design of 1985 was at first banned by the cycle racing authorities as illegal, but later became the basis of the LotusSport Olympic pursuit bicycle on which Chris Boardman won the 4,000 metres individual pursuit in world record time at the 1992 Olympic Games. Interestingly, as well as working outside the regulations, there are many features of Mike Burrows' design approach that are similar to that of Gordon Murray.

Like Gordon Murray, Mike Burrows is an enthusiast for his sport, and has participated as a racing cyclist. They both therefore have a very high personal motivation that drives their work, and both are steeped in the knowledge and expertise of their domains. They both constantly keep abreast of progress and current developments in their own and related fields, simply out of personal commitment, and this can often lead to insights and the transfer of technology from one field to another. A significant difference in working methods, however, is Mike Burrows' limited use of sketching as a design medium; he prefers to move quickly to immediate physical realisations of ideas in models and mock-ups. This is rather more like Kenneth Grange's approach of building models. Nevertheless, his successful approach to the 'monocoque' cycle design reflects Gordon Murray's approach of concentrating on a major objective and designing from 'first principles'. In Mike Burrows' case it was a concentration on pursuing the dominant principle of minimising aerodynamic drag, and being prepared to completely re-conceptualise the conventional bicycle frame.

A study of highly innovative engineers was made by Michael Maccoby, based on interviews with eight such people, nominated by their peers. Maccoby identified the life-long commitment of the innovators he studied, extending back to examples of interests stemming from their childhood or youth; the fact that innovators are not put off by failure, but expect to learn from failure; and that they have 'the courage to innovate'. He also pointed to several examples among these innovators of their experience of solutions arising from sudden illumination of problems that they had been worrying about. For example, like Gordon Murray's bathtime insights, the engineer-inventor Jacob Rabinow reported that 'flashes of inspiration come to him while shaving, driving, or partaking in other activities. Solutions are usually sudden.' Not all the innovators reported examples of sudden illumination, and for some, solutions only come from continuous hard work, but it is clear that sudden illumination (within a prepared mind) is a frequent element in creative design thinking.

Robin Roy interviewed the industrial designer James Dyson, who reported that he almost never solved problems by getting 'brainwaves in the bath', but more often when doing some practical work, 'welding or hammering something in the workshop'. However, this practical work may in itself be a way of letting the mind relax. Two of James Dyson's most well-known design innovations, the 'Ballbarrow' wheelbarrow and the 'Cyclone' vacuum cleaner, both came from practical experience and from drawing on technology transfer from other fields (rather like Gordon Murray's example of transfer of filter technology from medicine). The 'Ballbarrow' drew from Dyson's experience with balloon tyres on amphibious vehicles, and the 'Cyclone' drew from his installation of an industrial cyclone to remove fine powder from the air of the factory where the 'Ballbarrow' was being produced.

## Common Features

There appear to be sufficient striking similarities between these various studies of creative designers and other innovators for us to be able to draw some conclusions about common features of a successful approach to innovative design. We see in particular the immensely strong commitment of the innovative designers to their chosen fields of endeavour, based on a personal motivation that has been within them since youth. Added to this is a personal courage to take risks, even in the face of huge consequences for failure. The innovative designer is prepared to fail (occasionally), but is not afraid of failure, and of course seeks fanatically to avoid failure.

Beyond these personality characteristics, there are some useful observations to be made about the methods and approaches adopted by successful, innovative designers, and which might perhaps to some extent be transferable to others. A key aspect of the approach lies in defining or framing the problem to be solved, which is not always the same as 'the problem as given'. The goal is set at a high level, with clear objectives, and in direct terms which might even seem to be simplistic. It is this simple clarity which might make other people conclude that the goal is simply impossible. There is a holistic, systems view of the problem encapsulated in the goal. A clear concept of how to reach this goal is devised, sometimes by means of a sudden insight which comes when relaxing after deep immersion in the problem, and the solution details then cascade from the concept. Intense work is needed to develop, evaluate and refine the solution details; creativity is still '1% inspiration and 99% perspiration'. The clear, generative concept is not simply 'found' in the problem as given, but largely created by the designer; it is not a matter of recognising a pre-existing pattern in the data, but of creating a pattern that re-formulates the problem and suggests directions towards a solution.

This approach seems to require, or is synergistic with, a particular style of working. Some aspects of this style arise from the innovative designers' personality characteristics – for instance, their personal motivation means that they are steeped in their chosen domains, and they are prepared when necessary to work obsessively at their chosen problems and solutions. The working style is based on periods of intense activity, coupled with other periods of more relaxed, reflective contemplation. This working style may not be a reflection of a particular personality trait, but a necessary aspect of creative work, which requires alternating intense effort with relaxation. The innovative designer also likes, perhaps needs, to work with a small team of committed co-workers who share the same passions and dedication.

The working methods of the innovative designer are, for the most part, not systematic; there is little or no evidence of the use of systematic methods of creative thinking, for example. The innovative designers seem to be too involved with the urgent necessity of designing to want, or to need, to stand back and consider their working methods. Their design approach is strategic, not tactical. An important feature of their strategy is parallel working – keeping design activity going at many levels simultaneously. The best cognitive aid for supporting and maintaining parallel design thinking is drawing. Drawing with the conventional tools of paper and pencil gives the flexibility to shift levels of detail instantaneously; allows partial, different views at different levels of detail to be developed side by side, or above and below and overlapping; keeps a record of previous views, ideas and notes that can be accessed relatively quickly and inserted into the current frame of reference; and permits and encourages the simultaneous, non-hierarchical participation of co-workers, using a common representation. The drawing of partial solutions or representations also aids the designer's thinking processes, and provides a form of interactive 'talk-back'. As well as drawing, innovative designers frequently like to undertake practical work related to the design solution, such as building models or mock-ups, or participating in construction.

## Design Strategies

Three key strategic aspects of design thinking appear to be common across all these studies: (1) taking a broad 'systems approach' to the problem, rather than accepting narrow problem criteria; (2) 'framing' the problem in a distinctive and sometimes rather personal way; and (3) designing from 'first principles'.

First, there is the 'systems approach' adopted by innovative designers. From his studies of innovators, Maccoby suggested that: 'The innovator has a systems mind, one that sees things in terms of how they relate to each other in producing a result, a new gestalt that to some degree changes the world.' This sounds similar to the approaches adopted by Gordon Murray and Kenneth Grange. Maccoby continued with an example which might almost be describing Murray's approach: 'For example, one can think about a car in terms of all its parts working together to make it go ... In contrast, most engineers do not think in systems terms. They are concerned about designing a good piece-part, like a clutch.' This sounds like Gordon describing how his approach is different from conventional, piece-focused, engineering design. It also sounds similar to the approach adopted by Kenneth Grange, in his reperceptions of the problem as given, usually from the user's point of view, and considering the user's overall task for which the product is being designed. This 'systems approach' is evident, for example, in the way Kenneth designed the Frister & Rossman sewing machine so as to facilitate the whole process of sewing and the maintenance of the machine. Gordon Murray's introduction of pit stops also illustrates how a total systems approach was adopted – not just a focus on the design of the car, but on the larger picture of winning the race.

Secondly, the designers appear to explore the problem from a particular perspective, in order to formulate or frame the problem in a way that stimulates and pre-structures the emergence of design concepts. In some cases, this perspective is a personal one that they seem to bring to most of their designing; for example, Kenneth Grange has a strong, emotional distaste for what he considers to be 'contradictions' in design, where the object is not well adapted to its user and the patterns of use. As he said, 'My attitude is to want it to be a pleasure to operate.' And it was from operating the sewing machine that the new concept of an asymmetrical layout emerged, and the rounded edges, which gave the clients the re-styling that they wanted. In the case of the design of a hydro-pneumatic suspension system, Gordon Murray's problem frame was governed by his focus on 'How the hell can we get ground effect back?' in order to achieve his goal of the fastest car, while satisfying the criteria set by the FISA regulations. This problem frame led him to the concept of the hydro-pneumatic suspension system. For these designers, therefore, their problem framing arises from the requirements of the particular design situation, but is strongly influenced by their personal motivations, whether they may be altruistically providing pleasure for the product user, or competitively achieving the fastest car despite the regulations.

Thirdly, these designers either explicitly or implicitly rely upon 'first principles' in both the origination of their concepts and in the detailed development of those concepts. For example, Gordon Murray stresses the need to 'keep looking at fundamental physical principles' for innovative design, and in his design to regain ground effect he focused on the physical forces that act on a car at speed. And we saw in his city car design work that fundamental principles in details such as suspension and in manufacturing were part of his thinking from the very beginning. Kenneth Grange is less explicit about first principles, but it seems clear that he adheres to the modernist design principle of 'form follows function'; he approaches design problems 'by trying to sort out just the functionality, just the handling of it, and by-and-large out of that comes a direction'. This approach is evident in the examples of his product designs, which are based very much on the 'first principles' of function and usability. It was also evident in his design of the High Speed Train, which he based on aerodynamic analysis, and in both the big HST and the little sewing machine he questioned the established, underlying, standard engineering 'requirements' that had dominated the previous solutions.

Finally, it seems from these examples that perhaps innovative design arises especially when there is a conflict to be resolved between the (designer's) high-level problem goals and the (client's) criteria for an acceptable solution. Creativity is often stimulated when there is a conflict to resolve, and it may be that these successful designers recognise this and seek the stimulus of conflict. Such conflict is particularly evident in Gordon Murray's design strategy in Formula One, which was to challenge and, if necessary, somehow to circumvent the criteria set by the technical regulations. In Kenneth Grange's case, the potential conflict is often with the client's criteria for a product restyling job, whereas his goal is to provide the product's user with an enhanced affordance of use from the product. As he said, 'You are almost invariably brought in by somebody who has got a very elementary commercial motive … It's extremely unusual to be brought in to approach it from this usability, this function theme.' And yet, of course, the client's criteria still have to be satisfied.

These similarities in design thinking are illustrated in Figure 4.1. In each case, at the upper, systems level there is a conflict, or potential conflict, between what the designer seeks to achieve as the highest goal and what the client sets as fundamental criteria. At the intermediate level, the designer frames the problem in a personal way, and develops a solution concept both to match that frame and to satisfy the criteria. The designer applies that problem frame at the lower level, in order to identify and draw upon first principles of physics, engineering and design that help to bridge between the problem frame and a solution concept.

At the lowest level is explicit, established knowledge of first principles, which may be domain specific or more general scientific knowledge. At the intermediate level is where the designer's strategic knowledge is especially exercised, and where that knowledge is more variable, situated in the particular

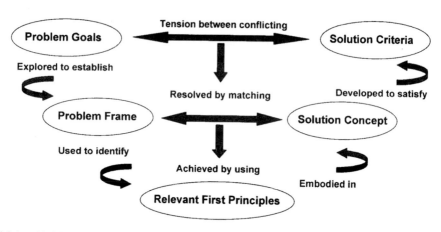

**4.1** A model of the design strategy followed by creative designers.

problem and its context, tacit and perhaps personalised and idiosyncratic. At the higher level there is a mix of relatively stable, but usually implicit goals held by the designer, the temporary problem goals, and fixed, explicit solution criteria specified by the client or other domain authority.

## Sources

Full references are included in the Bibliography.

Linda Candy and Ernest Edmonds: Creative Design of the Lotus Bicycle, *Design Studies*.
Bryan Lawson: *Design in Mind*.
Michael Maccoby: The Innovative Mind at Work, *IEEE Spectrum*.
Robin Roy: Case Studies of Creativity in Innovative Product Development, *Design Studies*.

# 5

# Designing to Use

In Chapter 1, I introduced the research method of 'protocol studies' as one way of studying design thinking in action. This experiment technique involves asking designers to 'think aloud' as they tackle a design task. The designers' statements and actions are recorded for later analysis, in which they are subdivided into short 'protocols'. The next two case studies are derived from these types of experiment.

Case study number 3 is of the expert, highly skilled, American engineer Victor Scheinman, who agreed to act as the subject in a protocol study. Victor Scheinman is an engineering designer with many years of experience in designing both mechanical and electro-mechanical machines, and robotic systems and devices. He was one of the first designers of modern robotic devices, and he has won several design awards from the American Society of Mechanical Engineers. He is an accomplished designer, outstanding in his field. Although Victor has a wealth of design experience, the design task set in the experiment was a novel task for him. The task was to design 'a carrying/fastening device that would enable you to fasten and carry a backpack on a mountain bicycle'.

This case study provides a detailed record of one example of Victor Scheinman's design process, in which his concern with product usability features prominently. Although the study comes from an experimental and artificial situation, there are some interesting observations that somewhat parallel those from the previous two case studies of expert designers.

## The Experiment

Protocol analysis relies on the verbal accounts given by subjects of their own cognitive activities. One of the most direct ways in which we can try to know what is going on inside people's heads, is by asking them to tell us what they are thinking. Of course, this is fraught with difficulties. People do not necessarily know what is going on inside their own heads, let alone have the ability to verbalise it. Also, there may well be side-effects of the verbalisation, such that it actually changes the subject's behaviour and cognitive performance. Or the subject may, quite unintentionally, give irrelevant accounts, reporting parallel but independent thoughts to those that are actually being employed in the task. These disadvantages weigh particularly heavily on the validity of protocol analysis in studying design thinking, where non-verbal processes are a significant feature of the relevant cognitive activities, and where the use of sketches and similar externalisation of thought processes seems to be fundamental.

Nevertheless, people do normally find it relatively straightforward to give a verbal account of what they believe they are thinking, or what they were thinking recently. Retrospective verbal accounts (i.e., recalling what one was thinking recently) offer one means of getting at cognitive activity which is frequently used not only in research but also in everyday interchanges, such as 'What were you thinking when you were doing that?' Concurrent verbal accounts (i.e., 'thinking aloud') offer researchers the hope that they really do externalise – or allow insight into – at least some of the subjects' cognitive activities. Of all the empirical, observational research methods for the analysis of design activity, protocol analysis is the one that has received the most attention and application. It has become regarded as the most likely method to bring out into the open, at least to some extent, the somewhat mysterious skills of design thinking.

For this study, Victor Scheinman was invited to participate in a research project into design thinking. He was told that the research would involve him undertaking a short (2-hour) design exercise, within his familiar engineering design domain. The experiment was conducted in a design room supplied with table and chair, drawing pad, pens and pencils and whiteboard, and equipped with video and audio recording facilities. Also in the room were a mountain bicycle and the backpack to be used for the design assignment. An experimenter was present in the room, and had a file of various pieces of relevant information and data that Victor could ask for if he wanted to. At the start of the experiment, the design assignment given to Victor was as in Figure 5.1.

## Design in Action

In the following analysis of Victor Scheinman's design process, quotations are taken from the transcript of his 'think aloud' comments, preceded by the timestamp for the quotation. After some preliminary remarks and questions, the substantive experimental session began at timestamp 00.15 minutes.

Quite early in the session Victor began to identify particular features of the problem that would influence his approach to developing a design concept. For example, commenting on the (deliberately rather poor) preliminary design that had been developed for the purposes of the experiment, and was available in the information store together with a user evaluation report on that design, he surmised that:

HiAdventure Inc. is a fairly large US firm (some 2000 employees) making backpacks and other hiking gear. They have been very successful over the last ten years, and are well known nationwide for making some of the best external-frame backpacks around. Their best selling backpack, the midrange HiStar, is also sold in Europe. In the last one and a half years, this European activity has suffered some setbacks in the market; in Europe internal-frame backpacks are gaining a larger and larger market share.

As a response, HiAdventure has hired a marketing firm to look for new trends and opportunities for the European market. On the basis of this marketing report, HiAdventure has decided to develop an accessory for the HiStar:

> A special carrying/fastening device that would enable you to fasten and carry the backpack on mountain bikes.

The device would have to fit on most touring and mountain bikes, and should fold down, or at any rate be stacked away easily. A quick survey has shown that there is nothing like this on the European market.

This idea is particularly interesting for HiAdventure, because the director, Mr Christiansen, has a long-standing private association with one of the chief product managers at the Batavus bicycle company (one of the larger bicycle manufacturers in northern Europe, based in Holland ). Mr Christiansen sees this as a good opportunity to strike up a cooperation and to profit from the European marketing capabilities of Batavus.

The Batavus product manager, Mr Lemmens, is very enthusiastic about putting a combination-product on the market, a mountain bike and a backpack that can be fastened to it. The idea is to base the combination-product on the Batavus Buster (a midrange mountain bike), and to sell it under the name Batavus HikeStar.

The design department at Batavus has made a preliminary design for the carrying/fastening device, but both Mr Christiansen and Mr Lemmens are not very content with it. The user's test performed on a prototype also showed some serious shortcomings.

That is why they have hired you as a consultant to make a different proposal. Tomorrow there is going to be a meeting between Mr Christiansen and Mr Lemmens, scheduled as the last one before presenting the idea to the board of Batavus. Before then, they need to have a clearer idea of the kind of product it is going to be, its feasibility and price.

You are hired by HiAdventure to make a concept design for the device, determining the layout of the product, concentrating on
- ease of use
- a sporty, appealing form
- demonstrating the technical feasibility of the design
- making sure to stay within a reasonable price range

You are asked to produce annotated sketches explaining your concept design.

Good Luck!

**5.1** The design brief for the experiment.

(00.22) it probably says the backpack's too high or something like that, and that bicycle stability's an issue.

He was also able to draw on some personal experience that helped him to formulate some of the implicit requirements for a good design solution:

(00.26) Having used a backpack on a bike in the past and having ridden over many mountains, unfortunately not on a mountain bike but I can imagine that the situation is similar, I learned very early on that you want to keep it as low as possible.

He then continued by calling for advice from others. In the information file held by the experimenter were examples of some commercially available bicycle luggage carriers and racks, including those of the Blackburn company, which Victor asked to see. But it seemed that Victor would normally also make use of personal contacts. He commented:

(00:33) All right here's what I would do at this time if – I would get on the phone, call up some friends. I have a friend who happens to have worked in the bicycle business for many years, and I would probably call him and pick his brain a bit. I happen to know that the Blackburn company is local, so I will call them up.

Victor telephoned the company and said that he was seeking advice about what sort of bicycle luggage carriers he should use for carrying a backpack on a mountain bike. For example, he asked:

I wanted to know what's the trade-off between carrying panniers on the front versus the rear, which is better on a mountain bike? ...
What happens if the centre of gravity is pretty high up above the bike, do you have a stability problem? ...
What happens if you put it in the front, it looks like you could put things high in the front, or is that worse? That's the worst, OK.

Within a ten-minute telephone conversation, Victor gained valuable knowledge of existing solutions to the design problem type, advice about the implications of some options (such as front versus rear mounting), and confirmation of some of his own prior knowledge.

He also drew upon his own personal experience to make the final decision that the location for the backpack would be over the rear wheel:

> (00.51) My first thought is, hey the place to put it is back here; there's another advantage by the way of having it in the back I can see immediately, and that is it's off the side in the front, and if you're on a mountain bike trail and you hit something you're out of control in the front wheel.
> (00.52) With downhill work on mountain bikes, I know you want to keep your weight back rather than forwards.

Victor's personal experience of biking with a backpack also led him to identify an issue that only someone who has had such experience might be aware of:

> (00.55) When I biked around Hawaii as a kid that's how I mounted my backpack … and I have to admit if there's any weight up here this thing does a bit of wobbling, and I remember that as an issue.

So the view that Victor began to form of the problem was that of the total task that encompasses the dynamic system in use of the rider plus bicycle plus backpack, and the issues of control of the bicycle that arise in the situation of riding over rough terrain with a heavy backpack attached to the bicycle. This is a different situation to that of everyday, smooth-surface, level-grade riding, and it accentuates the needs to position the backpack low and to the rear. The view that Victor had of the design task was significantly different from a view that might be formed from considering the bicycle and backpack in a static situation, or without considering the effects on the rider's ability to control the bicycle with a mounted backpack. Victor's understanding of the dynamic situation therefore enabled him to formulate a broad view of the design task.

From this overview of the total dynamic system of rider + bicycle + backpack, Victor identified stability as a key issue, and framed the problem as 'how to maintain stability'. Given that a heavy backpack had to be carried over the rear wheel of the bicycle, and given his experience of the 'wobbling' that can occur in the riding situation, this problem-framing and his prior experience led him to conclude that he must design a rigid carrying device:

> (00.59) The biggest thing that I remember in backpack mounting is that it's got to be rigid, very rigid.

He then developed this viewpoint into the requirement that the structural members of any carrying device must be stiff:

> (01.06) Making the carrier stiff enough for holding the backpack, that seems to be a big issue.

So, at about halfway through the session, Victor had derived a framing of the problem which directed him to design a stiff, rigid carrier, mounted as low as possible over the rear wheel. Having established a need for rigidity, Victor was able to utilise his knowledge of structural engineering principles as he developed a concept design for the carrying device – in particular, knowledge that a triangulated structure is inherently rigid. At this time, Victor began to develop his design concept through a series of drawings, shown in Figures 5.2, 5.3 and 5.4.

While sketching a rear view of the basic position and layout for the device (Figure 5.2), Victor commented:

> (01.07) One of the problems with a bicycle carrier where the frame is mounted out here and it goes to that, is that you end up with a parallelogram – bad thing, bad thing!

His knowledge of structural design principles led him to avoid designing a rectangular, parallelogram structure, which was the form that rather naturally seemed to arise from considering the basic shape of the carrier and the location of its supporting structure on the bicycle. Here we can see that Victor, like other designers, is using the act of drawing as 'a process of criticism and discovery'.

He expanded on this critical comment, emphasising his concern with stability as a key requirement:

> (01.08) If I were to make a frame that looked like this, that would be a very poor design because basically what I've got is, I've got a parallelogram which has very little lateral stability.

He then drew a triangular form onto the layout, introducing the structural design principle of triangulation, which offers inherent stiffness:

> (01.09) It would be nice if I could, for instance, run these rods up here to some point and therefore create a triangle, this would give me great stiffness – good idea!

Soon after, a secondary viewpoint emerged, which arose from considering the client's needs as well as those of the user (which had dominated Victor's thinking so far). The client for the design task was a manufacturer who wanted to sell the carrying device in conjunction with their already-existing backpack. The device therefore needed to have unique selling points that differentiated it from other, similar products. During the development of his design concept, Victor kept in mind that he needed the product to have a 'proprietary feature'. He used the client's requirement of a unique selling proposition to help guide and to reinforce his decision to seek a design based on triangular structures:

> (01.10) That is going to be our proprietary feature, a triangular, rigid structure with no bends in it; these rods are then going to be in tension and compression, no bending.

The principle of triangulation subsequently guided Victor's generation of the basic form and the detailed design features of his carrier. As he drew his design in more detail, he commented:

> (01.16) We're going to have this as a triangular structure here to provide the lateral stability.

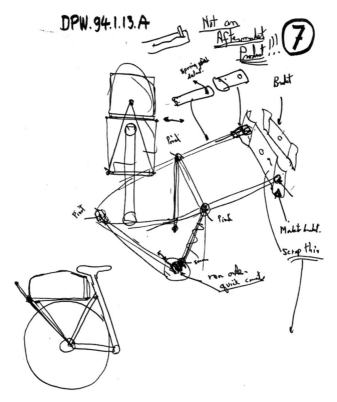

**5.2** Victor Scheinman's early sketch, in which he identified triangularity as a key structural principle.

As he continued to develop his design, he constantly referred to structural principles, seeking to avoid 'bad' configurations and to generate 'good' ones, making comments such as:

> (01.42) My detail here is going to have to be something like this because my forces along this tube are this way … good, this is good; and then this detail is going to be, er, let's see … all right that's bad, that's bad … that's bad, so I'm going to need something like that.

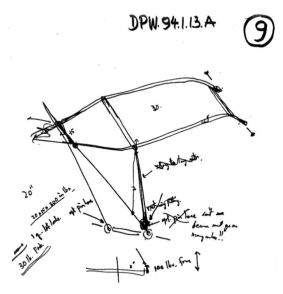

**5.3** Victor's later sketch, as he develops the overall concept.

At the same time, as noted above, Victor also used the client's requirement of a unique selling proposition to help guide and to reinforce his decision to seek a design based on triangular structures:

> (01.41) I want to make sure that this rod here comes to a point, not stop right there … that's to a point; that's going to be my feature.

In his comments, Victor demonstrated that he regarded the pronounced triangular form at the rear of the carrier as something to be retained as a feature that would help give the product an attractive and distinctive appearance. His design for the carrying device was therefore based on an integrated concept in which user requirements are addressed through the problem frame of stability, leading to the use of triangularity as the guiding first principle, which he then also used to address the client's goal of having a proprietary, unique selling feature to the product.

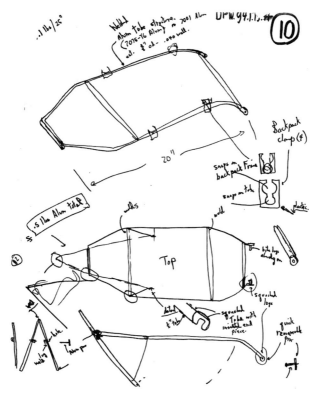

**5.4** Victor's final design sketches.

## Discussion

Having the benefit of a 'think aloud' transcript, we can see that Victor's creative strategy involves addressing issues at several levels of generality – forming a broad, system's view of the required product in its situation; from that, developing a particular perspective or problem frame for guiding the solution concept; using that perspective to identify relevant first principles of engineering design to embody the concept; and also maintaining in mind the satisfaction of the client's goal of a successful consumer product. This strategy seems remarkably similar to what we identified as common to those of Gordon Murray and Kenneth Grange.

First, all three designers develop a broad, high-level, systems view of the problem that they are given, in many senses 'going beyond' the basic problem and its initial narrow criteria. For Victor Scheinman the broader view was that of the whole situation of using the product, of the dynamic system of rider + bicycle + backpack.

Secondly, all three designers explore the problem and formulate a particular perspective in order to frame the problem in a way that stimulates and helps to structure the emergence of design concepts. Victor Scheinman used a distinct usability perspective in his problem structuring for the backpack carrier, for which, like Kenneth Grange and the sewing machine, he drew upon his personal experience of using such a device.

Thirdly, all three designers use the problem frame to identify basic design principles that trigger the origination of their concepts and assist in the detailed development of those concepts. For Victor, it soon emerged that 'bicycle stability's an issue', and so 'it's got to be rigid, very rigid'. Victor then relied strongly on the basic structural principle of triangulation to achieve the rigidity and stiffness that he considered important in the design of the backpack carrier. This led him to the triangularity of his design concept, which he then used to establish a distinctive appearance for the product, to satisfy the client's need for a unique selling feature. Victor's design concept integrated the user's need for a stable, rigid product with the client's commercial need for a product that had some distinctive marketing feature. As in the sewing machine example we also see here an example of how the designer's personal problem framing and use of first principles led to a concept that reconciled the designer's goals (on behalf of the user) with the more commercial goals of the client.

It is perhaps surprising that there appear to be such major commonalities between the case studies we have examined, which vary across real-world accounts and experimental observations, as well as across very different design domains, from racing cars to bicycle luggage carriers. But perhaps this does suggest that there are indeed some underlying, fundamental aspects that reveal the skill of design thinking.

# 6

# Designing Together

The case study in this chapter is based on the same experiment as the previous one, but provides a quite different perspective on the design process. In this experiment, a small team of three designers tackled the same design problem as did Victor Scheinman in the previous one, a carrying/fastening device for transporting a hiker's backpack on a mountain bicycle, and in the same 2-hour experiment situation. However, this was not a 'think-aloud' protocol study, but all the team's actions and natural conversation verbalisations were recorded for analysis. Because it involves teamwork, the design process in this case study has some strong differences from that in the previous study, and some useful new emphases emerge, such as collaboration and persuasion. Teamwork is of considerable importance in normal professional design activity, and has become of even greater importance as design becomes a more integrated activity involving collaboration among many different professions.

Understanding how design thinking operates in a teamwork context is therefore clearly fundamental to future development. The designers in this team were all experienced engineering product designers from the California office of an international, renowned product design practice.

## Teamwork versus Individual Work

Working as a member of a team introduces different problems and possibilities for the designer, in comparison with working alone. Some of the areas of difference can be surmised from the practical necessities of the situation, such as the need to communicate with other members of the team, and some others can be noticed from observation of the particular team recorded in this experiment.

An obvious difference from single-person work is that the team members have roles and relationships within the team, relative to each other. In a normal work situation, some of these roles and relationships may be formally established; for instance, there may be seniorities of position established within the team, there may be a team leader appointed by a higher authority within the organisation, there may be particular job roles.

Whether working alone or in a team, it would seem necessary to have to plan one's activities to fit within the available time. This may be easier for an individual than for a team, but in fact explicit planning of activities is not always evident either in individual or team work. Furthermore, it seems to be necessary in design for unplanned, ad hoc exploratory activities to be pursued when they are perceived as relevant by the designer. This particular team did explicitly plan its activities, but if unplanned, exploratory activities are a normal feature of design activity, it becomes interesting to see how planned and unplanned actions are handled within a team.

As we have seen, it is also normal, indeed necessary, in design to interpret and re-formulate the problem given as the task. The nature of design problems means that analysing and understanding the problem is an influential part of the design process. Individual designers can form their own, possibly idiosyncratic interpretation of the problem, but a team has to reach some shared or commonly held understanding of the problem.

Furthermore, in any design task, information relevant to the task has to be gathered from a variety of sources. A particular feature of the experiment design of this study was that information on aspects of the problem was kept in a file by the experimenter, to be given to the designers if and when they asked for particular items. This helped to make explicit and observable some aspects of the necessary gathering and sharing of information that any team would have to undertake.

Since a design task also means that the goal is to produce a design proposal for some artefact, it is necessary to generate some ideas or concepts for what that artefact might be. An advantage of teamwork over individual work might be that a greater number and variety of concepts are generated. Again, in teamwork it will be necessary to communicate and share such concepts and ideas. It will be interesting to see how proposing and developing design concepts are handled in teamwork.

A disadvantage of teamwork is likely to be that conflicts will arise between team members. Different interpretations or understandings of the problem may become evident, and different design concepts may be favoured by different members of the team. An inevitable part of design teamwork would therefore seem to be identifying, avoiding and resolving conflicts.

These aspects of teamwork will be considered here in the context of the experimental study, drawing on examples of how these issues became manifest in the team's design activities.

## Roles and Relationships

We do not know the normal working background of the team members of this experiment (identified anonymously as I: 'Ivan', J: 'John' and K: 'Kerry'). We do know that they all worked for the same design consultancy firm, had approximately equal previous design experience, and had similar job roles within their firm. We can assume that they were all approximately equal in the hierarchy of their normal work situation, and that there were no pre-determined roles that they brought with them to the experimental session.

However, it became clear from the video recording that different roles within the team were adopted. Some of this role-adoption was semi-formalised within the team. Some other potential role-adoption behaviour was not acknowledged and formalised within the team. Informal role-adoption is evident through repeated patterns of behaviour or types of comment by an individual.

This can be illustrated by just a few examples of the ways roles and relationships were established and played within the team, and influenced what happened. For example, immediately after reading the brief, Kerry suggested that they begin by reviewing the design of the existing prototype:

*K*:  What do we need? I guess we should look at their existing prototype, huh?

But John suggested a different activity – checking that they all share the same understanding of the problem:

*J*:  Yeah, em, let me think; we could also just sort of like try to quantify the problem, because, what's your understanding of the problem first of all?

This 'problem quantifying' activity (clarifying the requirements in the brief) was then adopted as the first shared activity of the team; Kerry's suggestion was implicitly overridden. Then, during the problem quantifying activity, Kerry suggested that gathering information from the user evaluation report would be a useful activity:

*K*:  They're not pleased with it so far, and the users' tests have some – in fact it would be nice if we could see those users' tests to see what the shortcomings were

Again, a suggestion from Kerry was ignored by the others. Shortly after, during a time-scheduling activity, Ivan mentioned use of 'information' in the context

of refining initial concepts. At this, Kerry again suggested that the user evaluation report might be a source of useful information, and again, this suggestion
was not acted upon, and was dismissed as irrelevant to the task in hand:

*I*:  Information or
*K*:  Yeah we wanna look at the em customer feedback or the users' testing
*J*:  Oh, yeah, so maybe, yeah, wherever that comes in, in this list

A little later still (and after meanwhile requesting from the experimenter the
information on the target selling price of the product), Kerry eventually got to
ask for the user evaluation report, but note that it was now with the addition
of Ivan's intervention:

*K*:  I think I'd also like to get the information on em
*I*:  The user testing
*K*:  The user testing

After the 'problem quantifying' discussion, Ivan suggested that they should
prepare a process and time schedule, and John and Ivan proceeded to do this.
Later, Ivan began to sort out the various documents on the table top, and
John took the opportunity to pick up on Ivan's interest in scheduling:

*I*:  … let's get this stuff sorted out
*J*:  OK you were talking about schedule stuff before, do you wanna
*I*:  Yeah, I think we should just figure out
*J*:  Just set some time limits for ourselves

Later again, when Ivan was planning the schedule, this role was confirmed
for him by John, Ivan adopted the scheduler/timekeeper role, and played it
throughout the session:

*I*:  Five-thirty we'll move on to the final cost and presentation, let's leave
      ourselves a little bit of time

*K*:  mm mm
*J*:  Ivan's gonna be Mister Schedule
*I*:  Yeah … on time, under budget

In these examples, we see that Kerry apparently experienced difficulty in getting the team to proceed in a way that she would prefer; that Ivan apparently accepted quite readily a facilitator role as timekeeper; and that John apparently had a strong influence on what happened in the team. These examples demonstrate some of the patterns of roles and relationships within the team that were evident throughout the session. However, these roles and relationships were not always fixed and simple. For instance, each member at times took a leadership role, although playing that role in a personal style. It seems inevitable that different 'role playing' behaviours will emerge in any team activity, depending on personality, experience, and the task in hand, and it seems that team members could be more sensitive to each other's preferences.

## Planning and Changing Activities

Within the team there was a consciousness of planning the design process; members of the team were particularly aware of planning their activities and of keeping their activities to a schedule. This may seem like normal procedure for a team, but in fact not all teams in similar situations construct such an explicit procedure as this team did.

Much design activity, particularly in the conceptual design stage, is unplanned, intuitive and ad hoc. Other studies of designer behaviour have made clear the 'opportunistic' behaviour of designers, which occurs when they deviate from current or planned activities in order to pursue ideas as they occur. It has been argued that opportunistic behaviour is appropriate behaviour for designers because it allows the flexibility to deal with design problems and the 'opportunities' that emerge in the design process. However, this creates difficulties in teamwork, where activities need to be coordinated, and an opportunistic deviation initiated by one member may be seen as irrelevant by another. In the analysis here we can observe how this team dealt with these aspects of both adhering to and deviating from planned activities.

Explicit planning of the design process was initiated when Ivan suggested that the team should prepare a schedule of activities, rather than just pursuing unplanned activities. Ivan and John then proceeded to list the following design procedure (Figure 6.1):

1. Quantify the problem
2. Generate concepts
3. Refine concepts
4. Select a concept
5. Design
6. Present

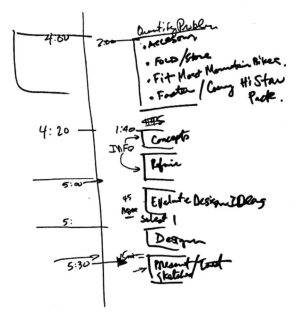

**6.1** The team's design process plan.

This procedure seems to be derived from conventional models of a design process. Ivan and John seemed to share a view that this is an appropriate design process to adopt, and this process was in fact broadly followed through the rest of the session.

As noted above, Ivan seemed to 'volunteer' as the scheduler, and at important points he would draw attention to schedule and time, for example:

*I*:  We have to start making decisions, we're already at five-fifteen

And towards the end of the session Ivan kept the time pressure on the others; for example:

*I*:  OK um keep moving along, we have fifteen minutes to finish our design

Ivan's role of scheduler/timekeeper appeared to be important to the progress of the team, and having a plan for their design process meant that individuals could keep a check on that progress and legitimately call attention to the agreed activities when progress seemed to be drifting.

Nevertheless, some activities were initiated tacitly, rather than there being an explicit decision to undertake the activity. For example, when Ivan suggested it was time to move on to the ideation phase, John agreed, but then began reading aloud from the brief in order to check that the listing of requirements was complete:

*I*:  OK shall we move into ideation?
*J*:  Yeah; I think we've, have we covered the, all the stuff ? I'll just read some of this out loud

Although they had seemingly agreed that it was time to move to ideation, there was no overt decision about how to do that, and in fact John began reading from the marketing report. While he was reading, the other two became restless: Ivan got up and went to look at the example mountain-bike that was in the room; Kerry finished her coffee, got up to put the cup in the bin, then picked up the example backpack that was also in the room and went to the bike with it; Ivan lifted the bike down from its stand; Kerry positioned the backpack behind the saddle. Nothing prior was said: there appeared to be a tacit agreement between Ivan and Kerry that they would work directly with the bike and the backpack at this point. They rather ignored John, who concluded reading and then went to join the others at the bike, and immediately entered into the activity.

John sat astride the bike and began to talk about placing the backpack within the central diamond of the bike frame. Kerry pointed out the impracticality of that; instead, she again held the backpack in position behind the saddle. John then suggested positioning it in front of the handlebars. Ivan began to record these suggestions on the whiteboard (Figure 6.2). The team had now entered upon an activity of considering alternative mounting positions for the backpack, but there was no overt decision made to adopt that activity.

One form of opportunistic deviation from a plan is a serendipitous shift of attention. For example, during discussion of weights (of the backpack, and of the product that is to be designed), Kerry asked for information on existing products (presumably to check the weight of comparable products). When this information was made available, it became more interesting as a source of design ideas, as Kerry indicated the structure of one of the existing products and Ivan realised the implication:

K: This looks a lot like the little backpack frame doesn't it?

I: Yeah; you see we've been, it seems like mentally trying to just, because of a similarity in size and shape between the two, thinking of ways to use the same product for the same thing but I dunno that we necessarily – I mean we're on a target for fifty-five dollars, I mean if they're able to make that for forty-two ninety-five … and if we just add a plastic part

This discussion then continued into talk based on Ivan's experience with a child seat on his own bike. These tacit and unplanned, drifting and discontinuous changes of activity mean that it is not always easy to track what is actually happening in teamwork. Some of the activity naturally becomes

**6.2** The team's early 'Concepts-positions' list.

more like a conversation than a formal debate, and topics drift in and out of the conversation.

## Gathering and Sharing Information

The experiment design, with its controlled access to the available information, meant that gathering information was a more overt activity than it might be otherwise. Relevant information not only had to be gathered, as in any design task, but also had to be extracted from its source and somehow shared among the team. In contrast to their rather formal approach to planning and scheduling their design process, the team had a more informal approach to information gathering.

The team relied heavily on any personal experience and knowledge that members had (or claimed to have) that was relevant to the problem. For example, Kerry used her own experience to offer an opinion on off-centre loading:

*K*: Well I've done a lot of lake touring and I've done front panniers and I've done rear panniers

[...]

*K*: Yeah, front panniers, you could, you could set it up so you could have one of these on each side – there's no guarantee you'd always have two – but it's actually not as bad as you'd think to have just one

During the earliest, problem-clarifying activity, we saw that Kerry suggested that gathering information from the user evaluation report would be a useful activity. Despite the difficulties she had in persuading the others to agree to gather information, within the first fifteen minutes of the session Kerry asked for, and received information on the target selling price, the user evaluation report, and the prior prototype design. For example, she interrupted the listing of the 'Functional Specification' (Figure 6.3) on the board by Ivan and John to ask for information on the target selling price when this was mentioned as an item for the specification:

*J*: Cost target, we don't really know what that is

*K*: Low

*J*: Low, but

*K*: Maybe they have a – do we have that information, let's see do we ask for – do we have any specification on what the reasonable price range is?

In the same way that a scheduler/timekeeper role was instituted, a formal role for an information gatherer/sharer might have been instituted by the

**6.3** The team's 'Functional Specification'.

team, but was not. Through her emphasis on information gathering, Kerry effectively might have been 'volunteering' to be the information-gatherer for the team, in the way that Ivan 'volunteered' to be the scheduler/timekeeper. But no formalised method for gathering and sharing information was instituted by the team, apart from the 'public' listing of requirements and concepts on the whiteboard.

Perhaps because there was no formal role assigned for information gathering, some misunderstandings and errors became evident. For example, there was no suggestion in the design brief that anything other than the specific,

'HiStar' external-frame backpack is the backpack for which the carrying/fastening device has to be designed. But both Ivan and John were confused about this, and Kerry had to correct their misinterpretation:

*J*:  OK I missed that
*I*:  Which part did you miss?
*J*:  … I thought I picked up that they were going to, that they were conceiving of making an internal frame pack, but I guess that's not what they're saying; you're saying that they make external frame packs currently?
*K*:  mm hmm they make external
*J*:  Does it say that they want to stick with that?
*I*:  Well it doesn't say anything about going uh external or internal, so that I think that you raised a good point, that we have that freedom right now
*J*:  OK maybe we could get something that we're gonna propose to them that if it has any advantage in this application, right?
*I*:  Sure
*J*:  OK
*K*:  But they wanna use it with this external frame backpack it looks like
*I*:  Right, with this, well let's see
*K*:  Because the HiStar, this is a best-selling backpack – the mid-range HiStar – they've decided to develop an accessory for the HiStar

Late on in the session, as details of the concept design were being resolved over a drawing, Kerry and Ivan forgot that a requirement mentioned in the brief was that the device 'should fold down, or at any rate be stacked away easily':

*K*:  What, the rack has to fold?
*J*:  Yes the rack has to fold
*K*:  Where does it say that?
*J*:  It says that in our spec
*I*:  Where?
*K*:  Our spec?

*J*:  Says right here
*K*:  (reads from brief) Should fold down or stack away easily

It also became evident that the team members could misunderstand what were apparently shared concepts. For example, throughout the session, Ivan and John made several references to the 'rooster tail problem'. Kerry did not query this until quite late in the session, when it became evident that she had not shared the same concept as the other two. She asked if they were referring to a particular tail-strap on the backpack, whereas they were actually referring to the spray of water/mud from the rear wheel of the bike onto the rider's back:

*K*:  We're calling this the rooster tail, this little tail?
*J*:  No, the rooster tail – when you, when you ride in the rain and it goes whoosh all over you

The errors and misunderstandings suggest that the team did not have a very effective strategy for gathering and sharing information. The fact that this was a short, experimental design session, and that there was relevant personal knowledge available within the team probably significantly affected the team's strategy. However, the reliance on personal knowledge, rather than public and more formalised knowledge sources, could again create misunderstanding. Even when information is apparently shared, misinterpretations and misunderstandings are evident, which means that common, shared understanding cannot always be assumed in team work.

## Generating and Adopting Concepts

Clearly it was necessary for the team to generate design concepts, and jointly to build those concepts into a specific design proposal. The team therefore had to develop initial concepts into more detailed and robust versions, and it had to decide to adopt certain concepts from among the several that were proposed.

A design proposal may begin life as a rather vague concept that has to have a lot of development work put into it. Concepts need to be built up, with additions and variations being developed to turn the initial idea into something more robust. There were many examples of this concept-building by the team members, co-operatively adding to and refining an initial concept.

## Bike Lock/Bike Stand

In this example, Kerry suggested adapting the carrier to be used also as a form of integral locking mechanism, and this concept was further developed by the other two team members into a device for supporting as well as locking the bike:

*K*: Maybe if you could flip it out and it becomes a bike lock, 'cos you know, lock up your bike while you go on a hike, that would be kind of a neat feature so you could justify some extra cost maybe
*I*: Right, right
*J*: Kick-stand alternative
*I*: Pull it around your tyre and now you can stand the bike up

## Shoulders/Child/Manikin

In this example, the team began to brainstorm from an idea that the carrier or rack device could 'wear' the backpack, and proceeded into flights of fancy:

*K*: What's kinda neat about their thing – it's not really a bag that this rack goes up inside, those um webbing details in the back
*I*: Right, that are already there
*K*: That kinda envelops it – it doesn't sit down on this, which we could add, but it's kind of a nice nesting feature
*J*: Maybe the rack wears the backpack straps just like we wear the backpack straps
*K*: Sure
*J*: (*laugh*)

*K*:  Why not, see, like you mount shoulders back here

*J*:  Yeah, yeah, just maybe, maybe you just mount a child seat back there and you give them a child (*laugh*) and make him wear the backpack

*I*:  Or a manikin

*K*:  A manikin … Harry the backpack holder

One concept appeared that was eventually adopted as the key concept that drove their final product design proposal – forming the carrier as a plastic tray. After generating some random concept-lists, the team then reviewed each list to eliminate unsatisfactory concepts and identify their preferred ones (Figure 6.4). One of the significant issues that the team had identified was that the backpack's shoulder straps, etc. could become hazardous if they dangle down into the bicycle wheel. As they went through their pack-to-rack connector subset list, a 'bag' concept was stressed as a solution for holding all the loose straps, and then the 'tray' concept suddenly appeared:

*I*:  We'll just call it that for now, er bag, put it in a bag, we're gonna need some sort of thing to do something with those straps

*K*:  To get this out of the way

*J*:  Yeah

*I*:  Yeah either the

*J*:  So it's either a bag or maybe it's like a little vacuum-formed tray kinda for it to sit in

*I*:  Yeah a tray that's right OK

*J*:  'cos it would be nice I think, I mean just from a positioning standpoint, if we've got this frame outline and we know that they're gonna stick with that, you can vacuum form a tray or

*I*:  Right, or even just a small part of the tray or I guess they have these

*K*:  Something to dress this in

*J*:  Yeah

*I*:  Or even just em

*J*:  Maybe the tray could have plastic snap features in it so you just like kkkkkk snap your backpack down in it

*I*: mmmm I was thinking of er

*K*: Snap in these rails

*J*: It's a multifunction part

*K*: You just snap in these rails

*J*: Yeah snap the rails into the tray there

*K*: mm mm

*I*: OK

*J*: It takes care of the rooster tail problem on your pack

*I*: uh uh, what if your bag were big, er what if you're on er, if this tray were not plastic but like a big net you just sorta like pulled it around and zipped there, I dunno

*J*: Maybe it could be part, maybe it could be a tray with a with a net and a drawstring on the top of it, I like that

*I*: Yeah, I mean em

*J*: That's a cool idea

*I*: A tray with sort of just hanging down net, you can pull it around and zip it closed

*K*: It could be like a window shade so you can kinda, it sinks back in so it just

*J*: Oh yeah

*I*: It retracts, yeah

*K*: You pull down, it retracts in

*J*: A retracting shade

*I*: Right, right

*K*: So that's not dragging in the spokes if you don't have anything attached

*J*: So what we're doing right now though is, we're coming up with like again classifications of solutions, kind of all, they're all either-or things, I mean like, we wouldn't do the net and the shade and the snap-in with the tray, either or any one of those will probably

*I*: Yeah, OK

In this 2-minute period, we see the key concept for their final product design, the tray idea, being proposed, accepted, modified, developed and justified. As well as securely holding the backpack, the proposed concept solved two

**6.4** The team's final 'Concepts-joining' list.

particular problems: the dangling straps problem and the 'rooster-tail' problem, which would dirty the backpack unless it is protected. The conceptual strength of the tray idea seems to lie in the way it embodied a potential solution form that, once it had been expressed, recognisably satisfied certain key problems and also recognisably could be modified and refined to accommodate other problems and requirements in a satisfactory way. Interestingly, when John introduced the concept, at one hour and twenty minutes into the session, it was the first instance of the use of the word 'tray', and from then on 'tray' was repeatedly used as the defining concept for the team's design proposal. The word 'tray' subsequently occurred 35 times in the last 40 minutes of the session, thus emphasising the key role that it played in defining the product design (Figure 6.5).

As well as co-operating in the building and refining of concepts, team members may find it necessary to persuade the others of the value of a concept they particularly favour (usually a concept they generated themselves). It is common for designers to become committed to particular concepts, even to the extent of becoming emotionally attached to a concept. There were two clear examples within this team of the need to persuade others to accept

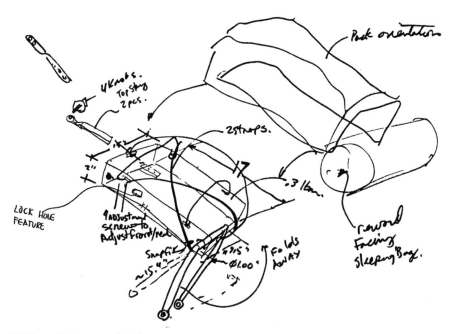

**6.5** The team's design proposal sketch.

a preferred concept. In the first, John persuaded the others that his 'tray' concept was the best to adopt; in the second, Ivan and Kerry persuaded John to accept the use of the fixed, brazed-on mounting points already on the bike frame.

As we have seen, the 'tray' concept was quickly adopted and discussed, with ideas being added to it, but John took care to ensure that it was added to the public list of solution concepts:

*J*:  I think tray is sorta a new one on the list, it's not a subset of bag

John also confirmed that he was emotionally attached to the concept:

*J*:  Yeah I, I really like that tray idea (*laugh*)

Later, when it became time to proceed with one preferred concept, John was quick to nominate the tray idea:

*J*:  Well OK, well we know we like this tray idea, right?

The second example of persuasion was based around using the brazed-on mounting points on the bike frame. This was strongly supported by Ivan and Kerry; John had some reservations, but deferred to Kerry's 'expert knowledge':

*J*:  I guess my point is, I think if you designed it specifically around mounting points, known mounting points on this bike, you might get yourself into trouble by limiting your market
*K*:  But these are pretty standard though
*J*:  The lower ones I would agree, but the uppers?
*K*:  That's pretty standard too
*J*:  The uppers are?
*K*:  It's getting to be, yeah, I mean it's not on this; but actually some mountain bikes are pretty scoopy and weird, but
*J*:  We can assume Kerry has expert knowledge

When it came to the team finally making a decision, Kerry conveyed her commitment and attachment to the braze-ons with an enthusiastic response:

*I*: We're gonna go with the rack, let's go with er, talk about braze-ons – these braze-ons?
*K*: Yeahhh!

It is quite normal for designers to become emotionally involved with their ideas; their design concepts are not merely abstract ideas, but personal insights that emerge as a result of some considerable cognitive effort. It is no wonder that these conceptual 'babies' are defended against other, competing concepts. This emotional commitment has to be recognised and allowed for in teamwork; creative design is unlikely to happen without it. However, team members also have to be able to recognise that some suggested concepts are just jokes ('Harry the backpack holder'), or half-serious ideas that are intended to help the creative process along and to which the originator has no serious commitment.

## Avoiding and Resolving Conflicts

It is probably inevitable that disagreement will arise between members of a design team. We have already seen that disagreement arose within this team over whether to use the existing brazed-on mounting points. More serious disagreement might have arisen if there had been competing design concepts to which different members of the team were committed. However, provided that a team collectively desires to reach an acceptable conclusion to their design task, it will have to find ways of resolving, or perhaps avoiding conflicts. In this team, there were instances where the team members acquiesced in a kind of non-committal 'agreement' until one of them found an argument that closed the disagreement, and where they postponed agreement and seemed to 'agree to disagree'. For example, a disagreement became evident over designing for adjustability in the rack. John proposed that the support legs of the rack should be adjustable, but Kerry felt sure that this was not necessary:

*J:* You know one of the things that seems problematic, and it would be great from a manufacturing standpoint if you could get around it, is this distance is going to vary with frame size

*I:* Right

*J:* But so, y'know, we were talking about maybe those legs could extend before so that you could get some adjustability on your rack, maybe you need that anyway just so that you can adjust to different rack styles – like a telescoping tube here

*I:* mm mm

*K:* I don't think you really need it

*I:* (*laugh*) OK

*K:* Because this is a twenty-six-inch wheel, or whatever, it's pretty standard and so if this distance – you're right it does vary a lot, but what's gonna change is maybe your angle on your rack is gonna change, what really is gonna happen is this is gonna be a fixed distance because if we go onto a braze-on or something down here, and you want to make sure that there's clearance here, and then as the bike grows it might pivot up a little bit more

Later, John returned again to the adjustability issue, appealing to the authority of 'good human factors'. Both Kerry and Ivan made rather non-committal 'agreement' responses; Kerry just shrugged her shoulders, Ivan said 'OK'. Their doubt was evident to John, who admitted that what he was suggesting was 'opinion not fact'. Ivan resolved the issue for the time being by suggesting that they can 'look at ways of making it adjustable' when they are finalising their design:

*J:* I think good human factors says it should be adjustable so that people can find the position they like
(*K shrugs*)

*I:* OK

*J:* um, that's my opinion

*I:* Whatever idea we come up with I think we can

*J*:  Opinion not fact (*laugh*)
*I*:  We can look at ways of making it adjustable

But the non-committal 'agreement' over adjustability was not permanent. At a later point John proposed a way of incorporating adjustability into the design, but Kerry came up with an argument that resolved the disagreement in her favour: if adjustability were necessary then it would feature in the already commercially-available products of the Blackburn company:

*J*:  One way to get that adjustability for the seat post height and all that stuff is if this, say this was a single bar and it went like this
*K*:  mm mm
*J*:  And it could slide along here, that way if you need to come up more, y'know pivots around the braze-ons if it needs to come up more for a taller person or for better wheel clearance or whatever, you just kinda slide it forward and put little lock-downs on it
*K*:  Yeah yeah, I don't think you need to change this length 'cos the wheel is fixed enough that you can rotate about the braze-on, and I mean if you really need adjustment I think all these Blackburn racks would have adjustments

These examples of deferred agreement or non-committal apparent agreement reflect normal aspects of human discussion and verbal interchange. But team members need to be aware of when they are close to reaching actual agreement, and when they are just deferring a committed agreement. Even when there is no overt disagreement, individuals may still nurse a contrary viewpoint and return to it when the opportunity arises.

## Discussion

The picture that emerges from this study is probably typical of normal team design activity. We have seen how the design process proceeds by sequences of both planned and unplanned activities; how frequently there may be mistakes and misunderstandings of the brief and external information sources; how the design problem becomes understood in terms of solution concepts that are proposed and developed in a mixture of personal and co-operative endeavour; how emotional commitment becomes attached to design concepts; how conflicts of ideas arise between team members, and how such conflicts are resolved or deferred.

It is clear that teamwork is a social process, and therefore social interactions, roles and relationships cannot be ignored in cases of design activity performed by teams. It is a collaborative process and, in this study, the conventional whiteboard and drawing paper tools allowed, and were used for, shared drawing and listing activities, including different team members drawing and re-drawing over shared sketches. This sharing of representations seems fundamental to collaborative design activity.

Given the apparent inconsistencies and difficulties in the progress of this design team, it is perhaps important to conclude with the observation that this particular group of designers was actually a very good team. They worked productively, and reached a relatively successful conclusion to the set task, within the prescribed time. Despite some of the observations made about the roles, relationships and social interactions within the team, there were no overt signs of frustration or dissatisfaction within individual members of the team. In the de-briefing after the experiment they reported that they were reasonably happy with what they had achieved in the available time, and that 'it was fun'.

In the next chapter we will make some comparisons of how the team and Victor Scheinman worked on the assignment in their different ways, and draw some general conclusions about working procedures within the design process.

# 7

# How Designers Work

In the previous two chapters we have looked quite closely into the details of how designers actually tackle a design problem. This was made possible through the use of laboratory 'protocol study' experiments that were in many senses far removed from the reality of everyday design practice. In this chapter, we will develop a broader summary and comparison of these two experimental studies, and try to draw evidence and conclusions about the way designers work when confronted with a design task. The fact that these two experimental studies have been the subjects of detailed analysis by several researchers will help to make the comparisons and summaries, but first we must acknowledge the problems and limitations of such studies.

It was clear in some of Victor Scheinman's 'think aloud' statements that he felt constrained in the experimental situation; for example, he referred to what he 'would do' in a normal situation, such as call an expert friend, but which wasn't possible to do in the experimental situation. (He did manage to go 'outside' of the experimental situation, and do something that surprised the experimenters, when he telephoned for advice from a company making similar products.) However, there were other, more subtle clues within the recordings of the experiment that indicated that we cannot rely totally on 'think-aloud' statements as records of mental processes. Some researchers have pointed out that non-verbal thought seems to be intrinsic to design thinking, and that the forced verbalisation of protocol studies must interfere with non-verbal thought processes. It was also clear that there were many points in Victor's stream of comments where his verbalisations stopped for more than a few seconds. On one occasion, he had to be prompted by the experimenter to resume his thinking aloud. Peter Lloyd and his colleagues suggested that 'it seems obvious that in these short periods of silence [Victor] is thinking deeply about something', and that these silent periods 'seem to be points of value where decisions are made, but we have no idea of the thinking behind these decisions'.

So we have to be careful about drawing very strong conclusions about deep cognitive processes from such experiments, in which a designer works alone and tries to verbalise his or her thinking. The second experiment, in which the three-person team of designers worked more naturally, although still within tight experimental constraints, obviously also contains many gaps in the individual verbalisations, where again we can make little assumption about what the individual was thinking. However, there are lots of useful observations that can be made from such experiments as these, and in fact both these experiments have been analysed quite considerably by a number of researchers.

## Collaboration

One thing we are able to do with a teamwork experiment is to observe how designers work in collaboration with one another. We have already seen in that experiment how the three designers tended to play different roles. Some researchers who analysed this experiment noted the different approaches to design that were shown by the three, and especially the differences between Kerry's and John's approaches. Particularly in the early part of the session, Kerry tended to want to gather specific information and to engage with the hardware and some of its details, whereas John tended to want to step back from details, work at a more general level of the overall process and gain a broad view of the problem. The different approaches of Kerry and John were summarised by Margot Brereton and her colleagues as wanting to pin down a solution (Kerry) and wanting to preserve ambiguity (John) (Table 7.1). Having two such emphases within a team can be good, but of course it has to be managed to avoid conflict and achieve a constructive outcome. Brereton et al. pointed out that, to resolve or avoid conflict, 'The designers masterfully invoke the support of neutral parties such as common sense, higher principles or theories, and expert or standard practices to support their opinions. These serve to depersonalise the debate, in addition to being means of persuasion and explanation of rationale.' These experienced designers seem to have had some effective strategies for working together that built on each other's preferences for ways of approaching the design task. Brereton et al. concluded that 'the collaboration is successful because the group is well balanced in their roles and manages their negotiation well. Kerry seeks to pin down solution alternatives, John seeks to preserve ambiguity and characterise the

**Table 7.1** Different design approaches of Kerry and John.

| Kerry: Pin down solution | John: Preserve ambiguity |
| --- | --- |
| Design specifically for the given backpack and bicycle | Design for various backpacks and bicycles |
| Focus on rear placement (most promising candidate) | Consider all possible placements |
| Design for a fixed position | Make device adjustable |
| Use emerging industry standard attachment method | Use attachment method usable by all bikes |

**Table 7.2** Different roles adopted by the three designers.

| Ivan | John | Kerry |
|---|---|---|
| Whiteboard manager<br>Arbitrator<br>Timekeeper – keeps the team<br>on track | Theorist: abstracts process<br>from context<br>Uses process rationale as<br>commentary to keep team on<br>track | Bike expert and user advocate<br>Seeks out context and detailed<br>knowledge<br>Seeks to ground the design with<br>specific solution alternatives |

ongoing process, and Ivan keeps the solution progress on track and acts as an arbitrator between John and Kerry' (see Table 7.2).

Despite the differences between the individual designers, analyses of the experiment have shown that their individual contributions to the session, while different in content, were often similar in terms of quantity. While John produced more solution variant ideas, equal to those of the other two together, all three contributed equally in analysis comments on solution variants, and John and Kerry each contributed exactly the same number of decisions in choosing between solution variants (Ivan rather less). Ivan, as we might now expect, made many more comments on organising the process, in contrast to Kerry who made very few such comments. Several analysts of the experiment have suggested that John was the most influential member, acting as team leader and being the 'ideas person'. However, this is not just a matter of being a dominant personality, and 'having the most to say'. Andy Dong made a very detailed analysis of the conversational patterns of this and other teams in similar experiments, and suggested that the constructive influence of a member in a design team is due to the way he or she interacts with the others and articulates shared concepts. He observed that, 'while John is a productive individual idea generator, he also builds upon Ivan's and Kerry's ideas'. For example, Dong refers to points in the conversation where John 'accumulates the discourse' and characterises a shared concept at that point, such as 'maybe it's a pack conversion kit' or 'maybe it's a little vacuum formed tray'. To 'accumulate the discourse' means not just to sum up, but to make a constructive contribution that focuses the previous discussion onto a type of solution concept and suggests a way forward. Dong referred to this as 'deriving a representation of the team's shared language that frames the design concept.'

However, in successful team design work, this constructive approach is not due to just one member of the team. Dong also looked at other teams and found that, in the more successful teams, the whole pattern of their conversation was more focused. A successful team's discussion showed more 'coherent' development, in which the team members built upon each other's contributions, progressing in a coherent form of conversation. The evidence for this lay in measuring how closely team members' contributions to the discussion followed on from previous contributions, rather than diverging from them.

An individual designer working alone has no one to collaborate with, so how does the work of an individual designer compare with that of a team? These two experiments, using the same design task, allow us to make such a comparison, and the question was explicitly addressed by Gabriela Goldschmidt. She pointed out that the cognitive tasks within design can be shared out between team members, whereas designers working on their own have to produce the full range of tasks of inquiring, formulating, suggesting, evaluating, modifying, and so on. She compared several key sequences of activity between Victor and the team, and found some significant similarities, with Victor's activities often 'shadowing' those of the team: 'He oscillates between overviews and technical details, between functional aspects of the design product and issues related to human factors. He thinks of features, product identity and aesthetics along with stiffness, strength and ease of production. Team members do the same, but they can let a colleague answer a question they raise, or pick up someone else's line of thought and build on it. The single designer has only him or herself to rely on, and he or she must act as a team and give all the answers while also asking all the questions.'

These comments indicate some of the complexity that there is in the task of designing. Goldschmidt's conclusion is that Victor implicitly 'plays' several roles, and acts as 'a team of one', as in this extract from his think-aloud comments about adding some plastic clips to his rack design, that would grip and hold the backpack frame: 'Why do we want clips? Because we want to take advantage of the fact we're using an external frame backpack. An internal frame can't use clips.' Here, she suggests, Victor1 asks, Victor2 answers, and Victor3 gives the design rationale. In this, there is an echo of designers 'talking to themselves' implicitly through their drawings and in their scribbled comments.

In both the individual and the team processes there is also an echo, and perhaps a confirmation of Donald Schön's characterisation of design as 'a reflective conversation', to which I referred in Chapter 1. According to Schön, this kind of reflective, or coherent, 'conversation' proceeds through acts of naming and framing: 'we *name* the things to which we will attend and *frame* the context in which we will attend to them'. He suggested that: 'In order to formulate a design problem to be solved, the designer must *frame* a problematic design situation: set its boundaries, select particular things and relations for attention, and impose on the situation a coherence that guides subsequent moves.' This seems to characterise well what we have observed in these examples of designers at work. The designers select features of the problem space to which they choose to attend (naming) and identify areas of the solution space in which they choose to explore (framing).

For success, these activities of naming and framing have to be balanced. Rianne Valkenburg and Kees Dorst studied successful and unsuccessful teams of student industrial designers. The successful team developed a sequence of five framing concepts during the project, in contrast to the single frame used by the unsuccessful team. And the unsuccessful team spent much greater amounts of time on 'naming' activities – i.e. on identifying potential problem features, rather than on framing and developing solution concepts. It seems clear that designing requires sophisticated skills in gathering and structuring information, and judging the moment to 'accumulate' and move on to solution generation.

For example, Henri Christiaans and Kees Dorst found, from protocol studies of junior and senior industrial design students, that some students became stuck on information gathering, rather than progressing to solution generation. They found that this was not such a significant difficulty for junior students, who did not gather a lot of information, and tended to 'solve a simple problem', being unaware of a lot of potential criteria and difficulties. But they found that senior students could be divided into two types. The more successful group, in terms of the quality of their solutions, 'asks less information, processes it instantly, and gives the impression of consciously building up an image of the problem. They look for and make priorities early on in the process.' This is the activity of framing. The other group gathered lots of information, but for them, the activity of naming, or simply gathering data, was sometimes just a substitute activity for actually doing any design work.

## Design Process

Experienced designers know that it is possible to go on almost forever gathering information and data about a design problem, but that they have to move on to generating solution proposals, which in themselves begin to indicate what is relevant information. In a design project it is often not at all clear what 'the problem' is; it may have been only loosely defined by the client, many constraints and criteria may be un-defined, and everyone involved in the project may know that goals may be re-defined during the project. In design, 'problems' are often defined only in relation to ideas for their 'solution', and designers do not typically proceed by first attempting to define their problems rigorously. Of course, this can mean that important information is overlooked, or is discovered only very late in the design process, causing disruption and delay. For these reasons, there have been attempts to set out models of an ideal design process, and suggestions for methodologies or structured approaches that should lead designers efficiently towards a good solution.

It is therefore interesting that, in this experiment, the team did set out a 'model' of their process and tried to stick to it. Their model process consisted of the following stages:

Quantify the problem
Generate concepts

Refine concepts
Select a concept
Design
Present

Some analysts have looked at the actual process that they (and Victor) followed. For example, Joachim Günther and colleagues analysed the individual statements in the protocols into three types, concerned with (1) clarifying the task, (2) searching for concepts, and (3) fixing the concept. Their analysis of what actually happened in the team is given in Figure 7.1. We can see that the three types of activity became considerably mixed together. Throughout the first half of the session there was a lot of iteration between 'clarifying the task' and 'searching for concepts'. What the team was actually doing through this period was generating lots of partial concepts and then considering the implications of those concepts. In that way they were exploring the problem through possible solutions. They did not spend very long on their initial task of 'quantify the problem' in isolation from generation of concepts, but after about twenty minutes they began to consider specific aspects of solution concepts, and then (thanks to Ivan) organised this into searches for 'joining concepts', divided into joining 'pack to rack' and 'rack to bike'.

The graph in Figure 7.1 shows clearly that 'searching for concepts' dominated most of the team's process, but came to a fairly quick stop soon after

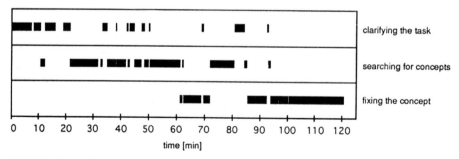

**7.1** Principal phases of the team's design process.

they identified the 'tray' concept, at around 80 minutes. Overall, they followed the activities that they had set out in their model process, but not in a strict sequence of separate activities.

It might seem surprising that 'clarifying the task' is an activity that recurs throughout so much of the session, as it did in the team's process. But this pattern has been found in other studies and is not atypical. Vinod Goel found, in protocol studies of architectural design, that 'problem structuring' could constitute as much as 30 per cent of the overall task time, and although it was concentrated near the beginning of the task it could recur constantly until almost the very end of the session. It seems quite normal in design work that there is an ongoing interactive exploration of both the problem and the solution, in the process of development that has been characterised by Dorst and Cross as the 'co-evolution' of problem and solution.

The graph of Victor's process (Figure 7.2) shows more clear-cut separation of activities, especially in the first half-hour, in which he concentrated on 'clarifying the task' by reading the brief and the evaluation report on the previous prototype solution, and telephoning a company that makes similar products. Victor spent some time in familiarising himself with the task, including considering his own personal experiences of riding with a backpack as well as collecting information from others. A concern with user issues was more evident in Victor's process than it was in that of the team. He 'internalised' the problem information, rather than making externalised lists (perhaps

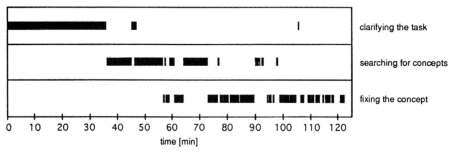

**7.2** Principal phases of Victor Scheinman's design process.

because he did not have to share and agree it with anyone else), decided on a preferred mounting position for the rack and implicitly on its material (tubular steel), and began a process of designing by drawing – making sketches of the bicycle and evolving a structure that met his user requirements for stability and stiffness (and the client's requirement for uniqueness). In fact, much of his design activity was similar to that of the team, in that he made progress by proposing a partial solution concept and then analysing its strengths and weaknesses.

Victor commented at one point that 'scheduling my time on these things, that's the hard part,' and he frequently commented on the time constraint he was working under. Organising a design process is quite a difficult task, because there has to be allowance for free-flowing activity within an overall schedule of things to be done within a time limit. The team's design process seemed quite complex; it was free-flowing, but it was also quite controlled. Brereton et al. concluded that 'the designers are continuously engaged in multiple activities at different levels. Although they focus in on issues, they continuously monitor the progress of the solution from the point of view of various requirements and solution alternatives. They reflect on their course of action, monitoring and modifying their process.'

The differences, such as they are, between the design processes of Victor and those of the team seem to be more to do with the differences between individual and team working processes. Victor was 'a team of one' and he was not subject to the pressures and constraints of working with other people, such as we considered in the analysis of teamwork in the previous chapter.

Some other studies have identified that designers usually start with a structured plan for their design process, as our team did, but frequently slip from the plan into 'opportunistic' pursuit of issues or partial solutions that catch the designer's attention, again as our team did. For example, Willemien Visser made a study of an experienced mechanical engineering designer who claimed to be following a structured approach, but Visser found frequent deviations from this plan. She noted that 'The engineer had a hierarchically structured plan for his activity, but he used it in an opportunistic way. He used it only as long as it was profitable from the point of view of cognitive cost. If more economical cognitive actions arose, he abandoned it.' Thus Visser regarded reducing 'cognitive cost' – i.e. the mental load of maintaining a principled, structured approach – as a major reason for abandoning planned actions and instead, for example, delving into chasing a partial solution at a relatively early stage of the process.

Raymonde Guindon also emphasised the 'opportunistic' nature of design activities, which was evident in her protocol studies of three experienced software system designers. Guindon stressed that 'designers frequently deviate from a top-down approach. These results cannot be accounted for by a model of the design process where problem specification and understanding precedes solution development and where the design solution is elaborated at successively greater levels of detail in a top-down manner.' Guindon observed the interleaving of problem specification with solution development, 'drifting' through partial solution development, and jumps into exploring suddenly recognised partial solutions, which were categorised as major causes of 'opportunistic solution development'. However, rather than regarding this opportunism as a weak feature of design behaviour, Guindon suggested it might be inevitable: 'These deviations are not special cases due to bad design habits or performance breakdowns but are, rather, a natural consequence of the ill-structuredness of problems in the early stages of design.' Like Visser, Guindon also referred to 'cognitive cost' as one possible explanation for such behaviour: 'Designers find it advantageous to follow a train of thought temporarily, thus arriving at partial solutions at little cognitive cost.'

Vinod Goel observed from his protocol studies of architects and other designers, that 'as partial, interim ideas and solutions are generated, they are retained, massaged and incrementally developed until they reach their final form. Very rarely are ideas or solutions forgotten or discarded.' Both Victor and the team worked in this way. Goel called this a strategy of incremental development. He suggested that 'a number of factors in the design task environment would seem to favour a strategy of incremental development. First, the problems are large … and cannot be completed in a single [problem solving] cycle. Second, since there are few logical constraints on design problems and no wrong or right answers, there is little basis for giving up partial solutions and starting from scratch. It makes more sense to continue to develop what already exists.'

## Creative Design

It seems especially hard in teamwork to follow a tightly prescribed process because individual members have individual preferences for ways of working. Also, for both teams and individual designers, there is often a natural flow to design processes that can run counter to a prescription for what should happen when. In analysing these experiments, David Radcliffe concluded that they demonstrated that 'the emergence of design ideas cannot be constrained to a particular place or sequence in a systematic design methodology. It is clear that design ideas emerge where they will in the continuum of the design conversation ... Ideation cannot be constrained to occur only during the pre-scribed time for this activity as dictated by notions of due process and proper sequence of phases in design.' As a specific emphasis, Radcliffe pointed out that the team's decisive 'tray' concept was generated during what was sup-posed to be the evaluation phase to 'select a concept'.

In analysing the team's design process, David Radcliffe spotted a potential weakness in their approach. They decomposed the overall problem into sub-problems of joining 'pack to rack' and 'rack to bike', as shown in Ivan's white-board lists of the various concepts (previous chapter, Figure 6.4). Radcliffe noticed that this decomposition of the problem made it difficult for the team to consider solution concepts that did not fit the decomposition. At the core of their problem structure was the concept of a 'rack'. At separate times both Kerry and John commented on the fact that the existing external frame of the backpack was in itself a structure something like a rack. Kerry commented that 'We've already got that nice frame on the pack; it would be nice if we can take advantage of that.' A little later, John commented that 'there's a kind of other class of solutions outside of our design problem [structure], and that's that you could somehow use the external frame and wouldn't need the rack'. Just a little later again, Kerry formulated a solution concept for a simple device, suggesting that 'maybe the attachment is kind of a leg that attaches right to the external frame.' Radcliffe notes that, 'Ivan records the concept on the whiteboard as "legs on frame" under the "pack to rack" heading … There is no explicit acknowledgement that this concept falls outside the pack-to-rack/rack-to-bike dichotomy. In terms of the recorded work of the team, listing concepts under suitably decomposed headings takes precedence over capturing less structured or controllable emergence of design ideas.' A 'no-rack' concept clearly does not fit anywhere within the team's problem decomposition. Although the team went on to consider some more ideas for such a 'no-rack' concept, eventually it was lost as they returned to their more orderly sequence of planned activities. This loss of a potentially radical, creative solution was precisely due to the team creating, and sticking to, a specific structuring of the problem.

Nevertheless, there did seem to be a classic 'creative leap' in the team's activity when John proposed that 'maybe it's like a little vacuum-formed tray', and this 'tray' concept became key to developing the team's final design proposal. Did the tray idea just come 'out of the blue' or was it an 'accumulation' of previous ideas and contributions? It was certainly the first instance of the use of the word 'tray', but some possibly related concepts that had been mentioned earlier included references to plastic as a possible material, and flat, solid forms for the rack device. In fact, nearly 20 minutes earlier than he first expressed the tray idea, John had referred to a similar kind of rack idea that he recalled: 'Actually a friend of mine suggested, a couple of years ago, a product that he would do, an injection-moulded rack that would kind of like fold down.' And Ivan immediately responded with recalling a similar bicycle luggage device that he remembered: 'It's like a little rack that was flat, it had these panels … but these panels were solid, it had little wheels … and it would come off and then it would be like a little trailer.' Ivan went on to explain how it worked when folded up on the back of a bicycle by over-drawing it on a sketch that Kerry had made (silently) much earlier of something very like a 'tray' on the back of a bike (Figure 7.3).

So ideas related to the device as a tray-like, flat sheet, probably of plastic, had been suggested earlier, both explicitly by John and Ivan and implicitly by

**7.3** Ivan's sketch of the 'convertible trailer' design, overdrawn on an earlier sketch made by Kerry.

Kerry in her sketch. The significant difference seems to be the overt expression by John of this concept as a 'tray' – i.e., a flat surface with a raised lip around its circumference. The strength of the 'tray' concept seems to be that it identified and summarised an easily recognisable, appropriate solution, in a way that was significantly different from the earlier concepts of a 'flat', 'folded', 'panel'. We can see that it drew upon those earlier concepts that, in retrospect, seem very similar, but that lacked the apparently critical feature of 'containment' that a 'tray' has. Its generation was perhaps aided by the immediately prior consideration of a more extreme form of containment, a bag. Like the bag, the 'tray' concept seemed to focus on one particular problem (containing the backpack's straps) as the most significant consideration, but it was quickly elaborated to satisfy a range of other problems and functions. John's expression of the concept was also timely – it came at the point when the team was trying to 'select a concept' and move on from problem exploration and concept generation to final design work.

To some, it might seem that John's apparently sudden expression of the 'tray' concept is an example of a 'creative leap'. However, our analysis has shown that the expression of the concept actually 'accumulates' a lot of prior concepts, examples and discussion. Creative design is not necessarily the making of a sudden 'leap' but is the formulation of an 'apposite' proposal. Once the proposal is made, it is seen to be an apposite response to the given, explored and possibly re-framed problem situation. It creates a resolution between the design requirements and the design structure of a potential new product. The sudden illumination that occurs in creative design is therefore more like building a 'creative bridge' between the problem space and the solution space than taking a 'creative leap' from one to the other.

In Victor's design work there were several points at which he clearly recognised breakthroughs or significant concept generation points, using expressions such as 'Ah-ha!' and 'Good idea!' Ömer Akin and Chengtah Lin analysed Victor's work, and identified a number of what they called 'novel design decisions': non-routine decisions that 'turn out to be critical for the progress of the entire design.' An example is Victor's decision to design a triangular frame, for rigidity. While there were 'hundreds' of routine design decisions in Victor's protocol, Akin and Lin identified just ten novel design decisions (NDDs), characterised by three features: an NDD resolves a problem or bottleneck, it does not follow from previous assumptions, and the designer identifies the NDD as an important feature of the overall design. Akin and Lin also sorted Victor's activities into three categories: examining (such as reading information, inspecting the available bike or backpack), thinking (whether verbal or silent), and drawing. They then went on to record the frequency with which Victor switched between these activities, and found an interesting correlation between the frequency of switching and the occurrence of NDDs. In almost all cases, they found Victor was alternating between the three activity modes in rapid succession at the point of reaching a novel design decision.

Akin and Lin were rightly cautious about drawing any inference that rapid succession between different activities actually causes or produces novel design decisions. Their observation was only that the two seem to go together. They concluded only that 'Our data suggest that designers explore their domain of ideas in a variety of activity modes when they go beyond routine decisions and achieve design breakthroughs', and that 'The designer appears to be decidedly engaged in all three major activities at the time of the NDD.' What their analysis suggests is that a designer's level of engagement rises, and they work across a wider span of attention to different facets of the problem and solution, as they sense the achievement of a critical, creative point in the process.

Some studies of student designers have also noted the apparent importance of frequent shifts of attention or activity mode in influencing either the creativity or overall quality of the design concepts produced. For example, in his protocol studies of industrial design students, Henri Christiaans segmented the students' activities into the three modes of gathering information, sketching and reflecting. He suggested that the more successful students (in producing creative design concepts) were those who showed evidence of rapid alternation between the activity modes. Also, Cindy Atman and her colleagues, from studies of engineering design students, found that overall quality of design concepts was related to more rapid transitions between different activities in the design process, such as gathering information, generating ideas and modelling. As before, there can be no suggestion of causality; simply flitting more quickly between activity types is not necessarily going to help a designer to be more creative. It seems rather that, in intensive design sessions such as these experiments, creative work is associated with a high level of concentration and engagement.

## Sources

*Full references are included in the Bibliography.*

Ömer Akin and Chengtah Lin: Design Protocol Data and Novel Design Decisions, *Design Studies*.
Cindy Atman et al.: A Comparison of Freshman and Senior Engineering Design Processes, *Design Studies*.
Margot Brereton et al.: Collaboration in Design Teams, in *Analysing Design Activity*.

Henri Christiaans: *Creativity in Design.*

Henri Christiaans and Kees Dorst: Cognitive Models in Industrial Design Engineering, in *Design Theory and Methodology.* See also Cross, Christiaans and Dorst: Design Expertise amongst Student Designers, *Journal of Art and Design Education.*

Andy Dong: The Latent Semantic Approach to Studying Design Team Communication, *Design Studies.*

Kees Dorst and Nigel Cross: Creativity in the design process, *Design Studies.*

Vinod Goel: *Sketches of Thought.*

Gabriela Goldschmidt: The Designer as a Team of One, *Design Studies.*

Raymonde Guindon: Designing the Design Process, *Human-Computer Interaction.*

Joachim Günther et al.: Investigation of Individual and Team Design Processes, in *Analysing Design Activity.*

Peter Lloyd et al.: Can Concurrent Verbalization Reveal Design Cognition? *Design Studies.*

David Radcliffe: Concurrency of Actions, Ideas and Knowledge Displays Within a Design Team, in *Analysing Design Activity.*

Donald Schön: Designing: Rules, Types and Worlds, *Design Studies.*

Rianne Valkenburg and Kees Dorst: The Reflective Practice of Design Teams, *Design Studies.*

Willemien Visser: More or Less Following a Plan During Design, *International Journal of Man-Machine Studies.*

# 8

# Design Expertise

At the beginning of this book, in Chapter 1, I set out some of the ways that the activity of designing can be investigated, and in the intervening chapters I have reported and discussed some of my own studies, and related these to the work of other researchers. In the main, my approach has been one of empirical investigation, based on reported experience or observation and analysis. In explaining and relating these various studies, I have tried to build an evidence-based understanding of how designers think and work. But presenting a description of how designers design has also been attempted in other, sometimes more imaginative ways. One of these is the use of metaphors or analogies that help to explain what it is that designers do, and the complexity of that task.

One of the most unusual metaphors was that used by Herbert Simon, when he likened the activity of a designer to that of an ant. Simon compared any creative problem solver, such as a designer, to an ant returning to its nest across a stony terrain. At any given moment, the ant's own horizon is very close, and all it can see are the rocks around it. To the ant, the terrain is not all visible in advance, and it cannot foresee all the obstacles lying in its path on its way to its goal. All it can do is deal with the obstacles as it comes to them – working a way around or over them. The ant, like a creative problem solver, according to Simon, is likely to take what would appear to an outside observer, with much more of a global view, to be a circuitous route 'home' to the solution goal. What Simon tried to communicate by this metaphor was his view that the apparent complexity of the ant's (or problem-solver's) behaviour is largely a reflection of the complexity of the environment (or problem situation) in which it finds itself, while the underlying cognitive processes that control the behaviour may be relatively simple. So in this view, understanding designing is more about understanding design problems than about understanding design thinking.

Christopher Jones used another metaphor of the designer, this time as an explorer, searching for a hidden treasure. Although apparently very different, this metaphor shares several features with that of Simon's: there is a definite goal, which will be recognised once it is reached; there is an unknown and difficult terrain; and the route to the goal may in retrospect appear to have been unnecessarily circuitous. However, Jones assumed that the explorer, unlike Simon's ant, has a significant intelligence. This intelligence can be used to help plan a search strategy, and to respond to any clues about the path to take that might be found during the search. Jones was suggesting that the designer can have a map, or a model, of the design process, to guide and control the search.

However, the metaphors used by both Simon and Jones seem to be wrong in one important respect. In design there is not an already-known goal; the designer creates the goal in creating a solution concept. If there is an already-known goal, then problem solving is a matter of searching for that goal, as Jones and Simon suggest. But searching for something that is lost is not what designers do. They do not search for a lost city or a buried treasure. Rather, they construct a fantasy city or magical treasure of their own. In a sense, they are genuine explorers, mapping unknown territories and returning with fascinating finds, rather than the searchers after certainties that both Jones and Simon describe.

## Design Intelligence

Jones was right, of course, in emphasising that, unlike an ant, a designer has a higher-level intelligence that can be used to plan, review, reflect, adapt and, above all, create novel solutions. What I have attempted to show throughout this book is that design ability is such a multifaceted cognitive skill. More than that, I have tried to show that there are particular, 'designerly' ways of thinking and working, that set design apart from other forms of cognitive skill. In fact, it seems possible to make a reasonable claim that design ability is a form of natural intelligence, of the kind that the psychologist Howard Gardner identified. Gardner's view is that there is not just one form of intelligence (as conventionally identified in forms of 'intelligence tests'), but several, relatively autonomous human intellectual competences. He distinguished six forms of intelligence:

- linguistic
- logical-mathematical
- spatial
- musical
- bodily-kinaesthetic
- personal

Aspects of design ability seem to be spread through these various forms of intelligence in a way that does not always seem entirely satisfactory. For example, spatial abilities in problem-solving (including thinking 'in the mind's eye') are classified by Gardner under spatial intelligence, whereas many other aspects of practical problem-solving ability (including examples from engineering) are classified under bodily-kinaesthetic intelligence. So in this classification, for example, the inventor's competence is placed together with that of the dancer and the actor, which doesn't seem appropriate. It seems reasonable, therefore, to try to separate out design ability as a form of intelligence in its own right.

We have seen many aspects of this 'design intelligence' in the case studies in this book. For example, we have seen that good designers have a way of thinking that involves operating seamlessly across different levels of detail, from high-level systemic goals to low-level physical principles. Rather than solving merely 'the problem as given' they apply their intelligence to the wider context and suggest imaginative, apposite solutions that resolve conflicts and uncertainties. They have cognitive skills of problem framing, of gathering and structuring problem data and creating coherent patterns from the data that indicate ways of resolving the issues and suggest possible solution concepts. Design intelligence involves an intense, reflective interaction with representations of problems and solutions, and an ability to shift easily and rapidly between concrete representations and abstract thought, between doing and thinking. Good designers also apply constructive thinking not only in their individual work but also in collaboration in teamwork.

The nature of design intelligence becomes particularly, and tragically, highlighted in rare cases where it is impaired through neurological damage in the brain, such as through a stroke. One of these cases was reported by cognitive scientists Vinod Goel and Jordan Grafman, who studied an architect who had had a seizure, associated with a meningioma tumour in his right prefrontal cortex, a region at the front of the brain that is associated with high-level cognitive functions. Before his attack, this person had practised successfully as an architect. Goel and Grafman compared his post-attack design ability with that of a 'control' subject, another architect with similar education and design experience, on being given a relatively simple task of re-designing a laboratory space. The sequences of design sketches that the two subjects produced are shown in Figures 8.1 and 8.2. Each began by making a survey drawing of the existing laboratory and its furniture. The healthy control subject then produced a coherent series of sketches, beginning with abstracted considerations of circulation and organisation, then developing proposals and

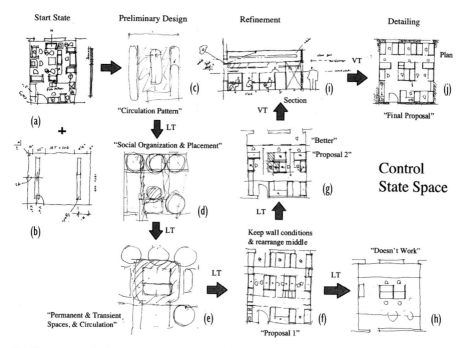

**8.1** The sequence of sketches made by the healthy control subject.

refining the preferred one. The neurological patient produced three separate, basic and incomplete proposals, finishing with a 'final proposal' that was still inadequate and incomplete.

The differences in the thinking processes of the two subjects become clear in graphs of the amount of time each devoted to different cognitive activities, as revealed by their 'think aloud' comments made during the experiments. These are shown in Figure 8.3. The control subject focused initially on 'problem structuring', with periodical returns to this. He then moved to 'preliminary design' and on to 'refinement' and 'detailing'. The graph of the control subject clearly shows a controlled but complex pattern of activities, with overlap and quick transitions between activities. In contrast, the patient

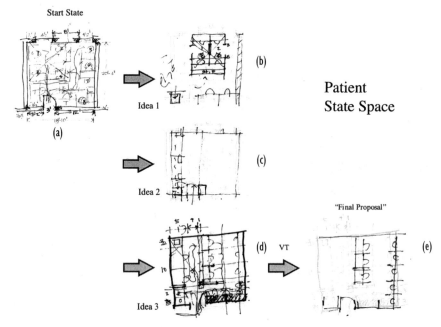

**8.2** The sketches made by the patient with neurological damage.

subject spent a huge amount of time on attempting 'problem structuring', and only small amounts of time on 'preliminary design' and 'refinement'.

The experimenters reported that: 'The patient understood the task and even observed that "this is a very simple problem". His sophisticated architectural knowledge base was still intact and he used it quite skilfully during the problem structuring phase. However, the patient's problem-solving behaviour differed from the control's behaviour in the following ways: (1) he was unable to make the transition from problem structuring to problem solving; (2) as a result preliminary design did not start until two-thirds of the way into the session; (3) the preliminary design phase was minimal and erratic, consisting of three independently generated fragments; (4) there was no progression or lateral development of these fragments; (5) there was no carry-over of

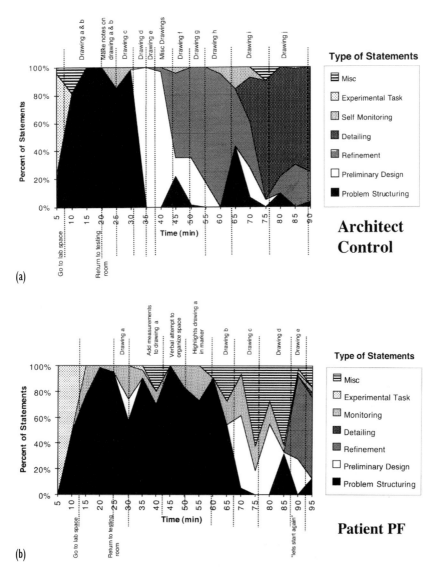

**8.3** The pattern of design activities as recorded in the think-aloud comments of (a) the control subject, (b) the patient

abstract information into the preliminary design or later phases; and (6) the patient did not make it to the detailing phase.' In short, the patient simply could not perform the relatively simple design task.

In this unhappy case we can see exposed some of the considerable complexity that there is in normal design thinking, and evidence that the brain has high-level cognitive functions that control or process activities that are essential aspects of design ability and that contribute to design thinking as a form of intelligence.

Studies of brain activities have identified specific areas of the right hemisphere of the brain as being active during design thinking. The two hemispheres of the brain, right and left, appear to have different cognitive specialisms. Neuroscience studies tend to confirm that the right hemisphere of the brain is more specialised in spatial and constructional tasks, in aesthetic perception and emotions. The left hemisphere is more specialised in language abilities and verbal reasoning. Damage to the left hemisphere often results in the loss of some speech functions, whereas damage to the right hemisphere, as we have seen, can result, among other things, in the loss of design ability.

A view of design thinking as a distinct form of intelligence does not necessarily mean that some people 'have it' and some people do not. Design ability is something that everyone has, to some extent, because it is embedded in our brains as a natural cognitive function. Like other forms of intelligence and ability it may be possessed, or may be manifested in performance, at higher levels by some people than by others. And like other forms of intelligence and ability, design intelligence is not simply a given 'talent' or 'gift', but can be trained and developed. Otherwise, what would be the point of having design schools?

## Development of Expertise

Education is not only about the development of knowledge but also about developing ways of thinking and acting. We are all familiar with the concepts of the novice learner and the expert performer, and aware that something happens in the development from one to the other. A novice undergoes training and education in his or her chosen field, and then at some later point becomes an expert. Education in design has well-established practices that are assumed to help this progression from novice to expert; but there is still rather limited understanding of the differences between novice and expert performance in design, and how to help students move from one to the other.

There has been more of a history of work on understanding expertise in some other fields and contexts, including chess, music, science and sports. From these studies, there is a general view that expertise can only be developed over time as a person matures. Usually, there comes a point when a peak of performance is reached, and then an inevitable decline begins. This performance peak will be reached at different ages in different domains: for physical sports, it may be around the age of middle-twenties, whereas in mental activities it may not be until much later in life; in the sciences, people seem to produce their best work in their thirties, while in the arts it may be in their forties. Some outstanding individuals seem to defy the general pattern of development-peak-decline, and to continue producing great work well into later years.

A universal aspect that seems agreed from studies of expertise is that it requires a minimum period of practice and sustained involvement before performance reaches a recognised expert level of achievement – at least 10 years from first involvement. This is not simply a matter of experience or exposure to the field of endeavour, but of dedicated application. One of the key factors in the acquisition of expertise is believed to be sustained, deliberate, guided practice.

The psychologist Anders Ericsson, who is an expert in the study of expertise, has suggested that 'The attained level of performance of many types of experts, such as musicians, chess players and athletes, is closely related to their accumulated amount of deliberate practice.' Usually, a young person may display a certain aptitude or interest, and parents or teachers then encourage and guide their development. But without the dedicated application of the individual, levels of performance will remain modest. Again, according to Ericsson, 'Superior expert performance is primarily acquired ... Many thousands of hours of deliberate practice and training are necessary to reach the highest levels of performance ... Most international masters emphasise the role of motivation, concentration, and the willingness to work hard on improving performance ... The masters seem to consider inborn capacities and innate talent as relatively unimportant.'

The development of expertise usually seems to pass through different phases (Figure 8.4). In all fields, the accumulation of experience is a vital part of the transformation to expert. For some people, the 'expert' level of achievement is where they remain, perhaps with some continued moderate improvement before reaching their peak and beginning their decline. A few manage to go beyond the level of their peers, into a further stage of develop-ment, reaching outstanding levels of achievement and mastery. At the other end of the scale of maturity, at a young age, all of us are introduced to a va-riety of human activities, whether it be playing football or playing the violin. We all improve a little, but some, as noted above, will begin to practise with a dedication – and probably a joy – that sets them apart.

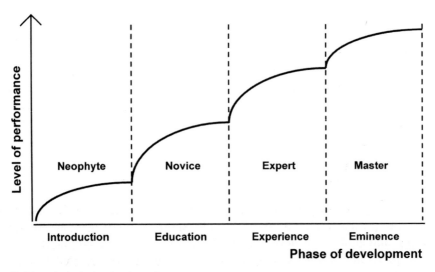

**8.4** Stages in the development of expertise.

The philosopher Hubert Dreyfus has outlined six phases of development from novice to expert and on to 'visionary' levels of ability. He suggested that a novice strictly follows given rules to deal with a problem, and develops to an 'advanced beginner' who shows some sensitivity to exceptions to the rules. Dreyfus then distinguished competent, expert and master levels of performance as follows:

> A competent problem solver works in a radically different way. Elements in a situation are selected for special attention because of their relevance. A plan is developed to achieve the goals ... Problem solving at this level involves the seeking of opportunities. The process takes on a trial-and-error character, with some learning and reflection ... The expert responds to a specific situation intuitively, and performs the appropriate action straightaway. There is no problem solving and reasoning that can be distinguished at this level of working ... The master sees the standard ways of working that experienced professionals use not as natural but as contingent. A master displays a deeper involvement in the professional field as a whole, dwelling on successes and failures. This attitude requires an acute sense of context, and openness to subtle cues.

Moving from one level of expertise to another is not necessarily a steady progression. It is not simply a matter of knowing more and learning to work more quickly or smoothly. The changes of level involve working in different ways. This shift to working in a different way can develop almost unnoticed by the learner but can mean shifts in level of attention that we all experience in learning a skill, as the fundamentals become performed unconsciously.

## Novice to Expert

Developing greater expertise generally means developing a broader and more complex understanding of what has to be achieved. For example, studies of novice and expert designers in the field of woven textiles found that the novices concentrated on the visual composition task and only occasionally jumped to construction issues to explore how the visual ideas could be realised in the weaving. In contrast, experts integrated both the visual and the technical elements of weaving, and generally considered them in a parallel way during the design process. Pirita Seitamaa-Hakkarainen and Kai Hakkarainen found that this iteration between the 'composition space' and the 'construction space' was a significant aspect of the experts' design process; they 'continuously moved from one design space to another to carry out very detailed processes of search for design solutions.'

How to develop such changes from novice to expert remains rather obscure. In studies of junior vs senior student design behaviours, Robin Adams and her colleagues found that changes in individual students' behaviours over the three or four years of their studies were quite complex and variable. Although there were identifiable changes in behaviour for many of the students, some did not appear to change their behaviours at all and some seniors simply spent more time on the given design projects but without any qualitative behavioural changes. It also appeared that some students exhibited different behavioural changes for different types of design projects; they were perhaps on the cusp of development from 'advanced beginner' to 'competent', showing more sensitivity to different problem situations.

In the previous chapter I mentioned how some student designers can seem to get stuck in gathering information, as a kind of substitute for actually doing any design work. A similar conclusion was reached by Cindy Atman and her colleagues, who found from protocol studies of engineering students that, for novices (freshmen with no design experience), 'those subjects who spent a large proportion of their time defining the problem did not produce quality designs'. As with the industrial design students, some of the freshmen engineering students, it seemed, simply became stuck in problem-definition and did not progress satisfactorily into further stages of the design process. However, with senior students, Atman et al. did find that attention to 'problem scoping' (i.e., 'adequately setting up the problem before analysis begins', including gathering a larger amount and wider range of problem-related information) did result in better designs.

In studies of problem solving, novice behaviour is usually associated with a 'depth-first' approach, which means that the novice identifies a problem aspect and immediately begins exploring its solution in depth. This results in partial sub-solutions that may be difficult to reconcile together into a satisfactory overall solution. The strategies of experts, however, are usually regarded as exhibiting predominantly breadth-first approaches – i.e., starting with a broad problem exploration and developing related sub-solutions together in parallel. Differences of this nature were found between the behaviour of novice and experienced designers by Saeema Ahmed and her colleagues. They found clear differences between the behaviours of new (graduate) entrants to the engineering profession and much more experienced engineers. The novices used 'trial and error' techniques of generating and implementing a design modification, evaluating it, then generating another, and so on through many iterations. Experienced engineers were observed to make a preliminary evaluation of their tentative decisions before implementing them and making a final evaluation. They used the foresight they had gained from experience to consider whether it seemed worthwhile to move further into the implementation stage of a design decision.

A more complex view than that of novices as depth-first and experts as breadth-first problem solvers has gradually emerged as more studies are made of expert designer behaviour. Linden Ball and his colleagues have studied the strategies of engineering and software designers and have suggested that 'experts will often tend to mix both breadth-first and depth-first solution development strategies ... the preferred strategy of expert designers is a top-down, breadth-first one, but experts will switch to depth-first design to deal strategically with situations where their knowledge is stretched. Thus, depth-first design is a response to factors such as problem complexity and design uncertainty.' This suggests that even expert designers will run up against unfamiliar problems, and will have to make some initial in-depth exploration of generated solution concepts in order to assess their viability.

One problem-solving strategy used by expert designers seems to be different from that employed by other kinds of problem-solvers, who usually attempt to define or understand the problem fully before making solution attempts. In common with what we saw of expert designer behaviour in our earlier protocol studies, many studies of expert design behaviour suggest that designers move rapidly to early solution conjectures, and use these conjectures as a way of exploring and defining problem-and-solution together. Peter Lloyd and Peter Scott found from protocol studies of architects and engineering designers that this solution-focused approach appeared to be related to the amount and type of previous experience of the designers. They found that more-experienced designers used more of what they called 'generative' reasoning, in contrast to the deductive reasoning employed more by less-experienced designers. In particular, designers with specific experience of the problem type tended to approach the design task through solution conjectures, rather than through problem analysis. They concluded that '[it] is specific experience of the problem type that enables designers to adopt a conjectural approach to designing, that of framing or perceiving design problems in terms of relevant solutions'.

Clearly, part of the development of expertise lies in the accumulation of experience. Something that distinguishes experts from novices is that the experts have been exposed to a large number of examples of the problems and solutions that occur in their domain. But a key competency of an expert is the ability mentally to stand back from the specifics of the accumulated examples, and form more abstract conceptualisations pertinent to their domain of expertise. Experts are believed to be able to store and access information in larger cognitive 'chunks' than novices, and to recognise underlying principles, rather than focusing on the surface features of problems. This kind of behaviour classically occurs in chess playing, where chess masters are able to survey chess board positions and recognise patterns, and strategies for resolving them, whereas novices cannot see beyond the next one or two moves. Bryan Lawson has drawn parallels between expertise in chess and design, and suggested that master designers also recognise patterns in problem situations and draw upon knowledge of precedents that they have abstracted into solution chunks, or 'schemata' as Lawson called them. A typical design schema for an architect might be a way of organising internal space, such as around an atrium, or for an industrial designer might be grouping together different functional parts of a product. Lawson also suggested that, like chess masters, design masters have repertoires of 'gambits', or ways of proceeding, of entering into and opening up the problem situation. A typical gambit might be like that of Kenneth Grange, starting a project by 'trying to sort out just the functionality, just the handling of it, and by-and-large out of that comes a direction'.

In order to develop expertise it seems that a novice needs lots and lots of practice, guided by skilful teachers. The novice designer also needs exposure to many good examples of expert work in the domain, and needs to learn to perceive and retain these examples, or precedents, in terms of their underlying schemata or organising principles. Like learning a language, it is a matter of immersion and internalising different levels of understanding and achievement.

Many of the classic studies of expertise have been based on examples of game-playing (such as chess), or on comparisons of experts vs novices in solving routine problems (e.g. in physics). These are all examples of well-defined problems, whereas designers characteristically deal with ill-defined problems. Some studies of expertise in fields such as creative writing where problems are ill-defined do suggest some parallels with observations of expert designers. It seems that some of the 'standard' results from studies of expertise do not match with results from studies of expertise in creative domains. For example, creative experts will reformulate the given task so that it is problematic – i.e., deliberately treat it as ill-defined – which is contrary to the assumption that experts will generally solve a problem in the 'easiest' way, or certainly with more ease than novices. In some ways, therefore, creative experts treat problems as 'harder' problems than novices do.

Just as design problems are 'ill-defined', so expert designers appear to be 'ill-behaved' problem solvers. Rather than the conventional behaviours of solvers of well-defined problems, designers are solution-focused, not problem-focused. This change of focus appears to be a feature of design expertise that develops with education and experience in designing. In particular, experience in a specific type of design domain enables designers to move quickly to formulating a problem 'frame' and proposing a solution conjecture. In various studies, successful, experienced designers are repeatedly found to be proactive in problem framing, actively imposing their view of the problem and directing the search for solution conjectures. Processes of structuring and formulating the problem are frequently identified as key features of design expertise.

In order to cope with the uncertainty of dealing with ill-defined problems, a designer has to have the self-confidence to define, redefine and change the problem as given, in the light of solutions that emerge in the very process of designing. People who prefer the certainty of structured, well-defined problems will never appreciate the delight of being a designer!

# Sources

*Full references are included in the Bibliography.*

Robin Adams et al.: Educating Effective Engineering Designers, *Design Studies.*

Saeema Ahmed et al.: Understanding the Differences Between How Novice and Experienced Designers Approach Design Tasks, *Research in Engineering Design.*

Cindy Atman et al.: Comparing Freshman and Senior Engineering Design Processes, *Design Studies.*

Linden Ball et al.: Design Requirements, Epistemic Uncertainty and Solution Development Strategies in Software Design, *Design Studies.* See also Ball and Ormerod: Structured and Opportunistic Processing in Design, *International Journal of Human-Computer Studies.*

Hubert Dreyfus: quoted by Bryan Lawson and Kees Dorst, in *Design Expertise.*

Anders Ericsson: Expertise, in *The MIT Encyclopedia of the Cognitive Sciences*, and Attaining Excellence Through Deliberate Practice, in *The Pursuit of Excellence Through Education.*

Howard Gardner: *Frames of Mind.*

Vinod Goel and Jordan Grafman: Role of the Right Prefrontal Cortex in Ill-structured Planning, *Cognitive Neuropsychology.*

Christopher Jones: *Design Methods.*

Bryan Lawson: *What Designers Know* and *How Designers Think.*

Peter Lloyd and Peter Scott: Difference in Similarity, *Planning and Design.*

Pirita Seitamaa-Hakkarainen and Kai Hakkarainen: Composition and Construction in Experts' and Novices' Weaving Design, *Design Studies*.

Herbert Simon: *The Sciences of the Artificial*.

# Bibliography

Adams, R., Turns, J. and Atman, C. (2003) Educating Effective Engineering Designers: The Role of Reflective Practice, *Design Studies*, Vol. 24, 275–294

Ahmed, S., Wallace, K. and Blessing, L. (2003) Understanding the Differences Between How Novice and Experienced Designers Approach Design Tasks, *Research in Engineering Design*, Vol. 14, 1–11

Akin, Ö. and Lin, C. (1995) Design Protocol Data and Novel Design Decisions, *Design Studies,* Vol. 16, 211–236, and in Cross, N., Christiaans, H. and Dorst, K. (eds) *Analysing Design Activity*, Chichester: Wiley

Atman, C., Cardella, M., Turns, J. and Adams, R. (2005) Comparing Freshman and Senior Engineering Design Processes: An In-depth Follow-up Study, *Design Studies*, Vol. 26, 325–357

Atman, C., Chimka, J., Bursic, K. and Nachtman, H. (1999) A Comparison of Freshman and Senior Engineering Design Processes, *Design Studies*, Vol. 20, 131–152

Ball, L. and Ormerod, T. (1995) Structured and Opportunistic Processing in Design: A Critical

Discussion, *International Journal of Human-Computer Studies*, Vol. 43, 131–151

Ball, L., Onarheim, B. and Christensen, B. (2010) Design Requirements, Epistemic Uncertainty and Solution Development Strategies in Software Design, *Design Studies*, Vol. 31, 567–589

Brereton, M., Cannon, D., Mabogunje, A., and Leifer, L. (1996) Collaboration in Design Teams: How Social Interaction Shapes the Product, in N. Cross, H. Christiaans and K. Dorst (eds) *Analysing Design Activity*, Chichester: Wiley

Bucciarelli, L. (1994) *Designing Engineers*, Cambridge, MA: MIT Press

Candy, L. and Edmonds, E. (1996) Creative Design of the Lotus Bicycle, *Design Studies*, Vol. 17, 71–90

Christiaans, H. (1992) *Creativity in Design: The Role of Domain Knowledge in Design*, Utrecht: Lemma

Christiaans, H. and Dorst, K. (1992) Cognitive Models in Industrial Design Engineering: A Protocol Study, in D. Taylor and D. Stauffer (eds), *Design Theory and Methodology*, New York: American Society of Mechanical Engineers

Cross, N., Christiaans, H. and Dorst, K. (1994) Design Expertise Amongst Student Designers, *Journal of Art and Design Education*, Vol. 13, 39–56

Cross, N., Christiaans, H. and Dorst, K. (eds) (1996) *Analysing Design Activity*, Chichester: Wiley

Darke, J. (1979) The Primary Generator and the Design Process, *Design Studies*, Vol. 1, 36–44

Davies, R. (1985) A Psychological Enquiry into the Origination and Implementation of Ideas, MSc Thesis, Department of Management Sciences, University of Manchester

Davies, R. and Talbot, R. (1987) Experiencing Ideas: Identity, Insight and the Imago, *Design Studies*, Vol. 8, 17–25

Dong, A. (2005) The Latent Semantic Approach to Studying Design Team Communication, *Design Studies*, Vol. 26, 445–461

Dorst, K. and Cross, N. (2001) Creativity in the Design Process: Co-evolution of Problem-solution, *Design Studies*, Vol. 22, 425–437

Dreyfus, H., quoted in B. Lawson and K. Dorst (2009) *Design Expertise*, Oxford: Architectural Press/Elsevier

Ericsson, K. A. (1999) Expertise, in R. Wilson and F. Keil (eds) *The MIT Encyclopedia of the Cognitive Sciences*, Cambridge, MA: MIT Press

Ericsson, K. A. (2001) Attaining Excellence Through Deliberate Practice: Insights from the Study of

Expert Performance, in M. Ferrari
(ed.), *The Pursuit of Excellence
Through Education*, Hillsdale, NJ:
Erlbaum

Gardner, H. (1983) *Frames of Mind:
The Theory of Multiple Intelligences*,
London: Heinemann

Gedenryd, H. (1998) How Designers
Work, PhD Thesis, Department of
Cognitive Science, Lund University,
Sweden

Goel, V. (1995) *Sketches of Thought*,
Cambridge, MA: MIT Press

Goel, V. and Grafman, J. (2000) Role
of the Right Prefrontal Cortex in
Ill-structured Planning, *Cognitive
Neuropsychology*, Vol. 17, 415–436

Goldschmidt, G. (1995) The Designer
as a Team of One, *Design Studies*,
Vol. 16, 189–209, and in N. Cross,
H. Christiaans and K. Dorst
(eds) *Analysing Design Activity*,
Chichester: Wiley

Guindon, R. (1990) Designing the Design
Process: Exploiting Opportunistic
Thoughts, *Human-Computer
Interaction,* Vol. 5, 305–344

Günther, J., Frankenberger, E. and Auer,
P. (1996) Investigation of Individual
and Team Design Processes, in N.
Cross, H. Christiaans and K. Dorst
(eds), *Analysing Design Activity*,
Chichester: Wiley

Jones, J. C. (1992) *Design Methods*,
Chichester: Wiley

Lawson, B. (1994) *Design In Mind*,
Oxford: Butterworth-Heinemann

Lawson, B. (2004) *What Designers
Know*, Oxford: Architectural Press/
Elsevier

Lawson, B. (2006) *How Designers
Think*, Oxford: Architectural Press/
Elsevier

Levin, P. (1966) *Decision Making in
Urban Design*, Watford, UK: Building
Research Establishment

Lloyd, P., Lawson, B. and Scott, P. (1995)
Can Concurrent Verbalization Reveal
Design Cognition? *Design Studies,*
Vol. 16, 237–259, and in N. Cross,
H. Christiaans and K. Dorst (eds)
(1996), *Analysing Design Activity*,
Chichester: Wiley

Lloyd, P. and Scott, P. (1995) Difference
in Similarity: Interpreting the
Architectural Design Process,
*Planning and Design*, Vol. 22,
383–406

Lloyd, P. and Snelders, D. (2003) What
was Philippe Starck thinking of?
*Design Studies*, Vol. 24, 237–253

Maccoby, M. (1991) The Innovative Mind
at Work, *IEEE Spectrum*, December,
23–35

March, L. (1976) The Logic of Design,
in *The Architecture of Form*,
Cambridge: Cambridge University
Press

Murray, D. (1993) An Ethnographic
Study of Graphic Designers, in G.

de Michelis and C. Simone (eds),
*European Conference on Computer
Supported Cooperative Work*,
Dordrecht: Kluwer

Radcliffe, D. (1996) Concurrency
of Actions, Ideas and Knowledge
Displays Within a Design Team, in N.
Cross, H. Christiaans and K. Dorst
(eds), *Analysing Design Activity*,
Chichester: Wiley

Rowe, P. (1987) *Design Thinking*,
Cambridge, MA: MIT Press

Roy, R. (1993) Case Studies of Creativity
in Innovative Product Development,
*Design Studies*, Vol. 14, 423–443

Schön, D. (1983) *The Reflective
Practitioner: How Professionals
Think in Action*, New York: Basic
Books

Schön, D. (1988) Designing: Rules, Types
and Worlds, *Design Studies*, Vol. 9,
181–190

Seitamaa-Hakkarainen, P. and
Hakkarainen, K. (2001) Composition
and Construction in Experts' and
Novices' Weaving Design, *Design
Studies*, Vol. 22, 47–66

Simon, H. (1969) *The Sciences of the
Artificial*, Cambridge, MA: MIT
Press

Valkenburg, R. and Dorst, K. (1998) The
Reflective Practice of Design Teams,
*Design Studies*, Vol. 19, 249–271

Visser, W. (1990) More or Less Following
a Plan During Design: Opportunistic
Deviations in Specification,
*International Journal of Man-
Machine Studies*, Vol. 33, 247–278

# Illustration Credits

## Chapter 1

Figure 1.1 courtesy of Philippe Starck. Photograph by Nigel Cross.
Figure 1.3 courtesy of Philippe Starck.

## Chapter 2

Figure 2.1 courtesy of McLaren Automotive.
Figure 2.2 courtesy of Gordon Murray/McLaren Automotive.
Figure 2.3 courtesy of Gordon Murray.
Figure 2.4 courtesy of Gordon Murray.
Figure 2.5 courtesy of Gordon Murray.
Figure 2.6 courtesy of Gordon Murray. Photograph by Nigel Cross.
Figure 2.7 courtesy of Gordon Murray.

# Chapter 3

Figure 3.1 courtesy of Kenneth Grange.
Figure 3.2 courtesy of Kenneth Grange.
Figure 3.3 courtesy of Kenneth Grange.

# Chapter 5

Figure 5.2 courtesy of Wiley-Blackwell, Victor Scheinman.
Figure 5.3 courtesy of Wiley-Blackwell, Victor Scheinman.
Figure 5.4 courtesy of Wiley-Blackwell, Victor Scheinman.

# Chapter 6

Figure 6.1 courtesy of Wiley-Blackwell, 'Ivan, John and Kerry'.
Figure 6.2 courtesy of Wiley-Blackwell, 'Ivan, John and Kerry'.
Figure 6.3 courtesy of Wiley-Blackwell, 'Ivan, John and Kerry'.
Figure 6.4 courtesy of Wiley-Blackwell, 'Ivan, John and Kerry'.
Figure 6.5 courtesy of Wiley-Blackwell, 'Ivan, John and Kerry'.

# Chapter 7

Figure 7.1 courtesy of Wiley-Blackwell, Joachim Günter, Eckart Frankenberger and Peter Auer.
Figure 7.2 courtesy of Wiley-Blackwell, Joachim Günter, Eckart Frankenberger and Peter Auer.
Figure 7.3 courtesy of Wiley-Blackwell, 'Ivan, John and Kerry'.

## Chapter 8

Figure 8.1 courtesy of Taylor & Francis Group (www.informaworld.com), *Cognitive Neuropsychology*, Vinod Goel and Jordan Grafman.
Figure 8.2 courtesy of Taylor & Francis Group (www.informaworld.com), *Cognitive Neuropsychology*, Vinod Goel and Jordan Grafman.
Figure 8.3 courtesy of Taylor & Francis Group (www.informaworld.com), *Cognitive Neuropsychology*, Vinod Goel and Jordan Grafman.

# Index